CONFLICT
and CREATIVITY
at WORK

Conflict and Creativity at Work
Human Roots of Corporate Life

is the follow-up to Albert Low's *Zen and Creative Management*, which was first published in 1976 and sold 75,000 copies.

Endorsements for *Zen and Creative Management*

"His insight and integrity is exactly the message that business leaders need to hear — particularly business leaders who seek to define a new way of working, competing, and succeeding . . . I featured his book in an early issue of *Fast Company*. In my view, the course of business in the last seven years has only confirmed Albert's philosophy . . . A remarkable contribution to the discourse on business, work, and meaning." Alan Weber, one time senior editor of the *Harvard Business Review,* and the founding editor of the magazine *Fast Company*

"*Zen and Creative Management* is a must for managers whose objectives are to improve conditions in the workplace and to increase productivity. It offers all managers a wide range of innovative ways to analyze long-term priorities and day-to-day operations, and suggests methods to implement change." Elliott Jaques, author of *Requisite Organization: Total System for Effective Managerial Organization and Managerial Leadership for the 21st Century*

"Albert Low has written an original and important book on management. It combines Western and Eastern modes of thought to construct an intensely practical and flexible approach to the solution of managerial problems." Philip Kapleau, author of *The Three Pillars of Zen*

"In planning today the problem is how to head off and control effects by anticipating them. Men have always tended to be servants of their technologies. *Zen and Creative Management* suggests ways of bypassing this fate." Marshall McLuhan

And endorsements for *Conflict and Creativity at Work* are equally engaging:

"Albert Low has spent a lifetime searching for the foundations of harmony and creative satisfaction in common human endeavors — inside and outside the corporation. His questions are timely for all executives to consider." Kathryn Cason, Co-founder and President, Requisite Organization International Institute (ROII)

"Great management calls for fundamental and keen awareness, of the sort that is easy to recognize — and very hard to teach. Albert Low, in an easy-going, straightforward, low-key and respectful way, provides that education in the context of corporate purpose. This is an erudite book, not opaque or academic, but thoughtful and intent on getting its readers through the looking glass of personal and organizational change." Art Kleiner, Editor-in-chief, strategy+business, and author of *The Age of Heretics*

"Albert Low raises thought-provoking questions and ethical considerations that are important for the management field to consider. Elliott Jaques argued that the beginning of any science starts with the development of clearly articulated concepts that have only one unequivocal meaning. Albert Low in *Conflict and Creativity at Work* is willing to engage in the discussion of the meaning of foundational concepts in the management field that Elliott Jaques began over 60 years ago. It is a pleasure to read work that reflects the importance of that discussion." Alison Brause, Business consultant and Board Member, Requisite Organization International Institute (ROII)

"For more than a century, management thinkers have treated human consciousness as a black box, conveniently ignoring its role in the creation and management of a company. Albert Low takes us on a journey that will forever change our conceptions of organizations, work and the role of human creativity in making organizations sustainable and ethical organisms in the global ecosystem . . . For those tired of same old management books that offer pat answers and platitudes, this is a book worth pondering and cherishing for decades to come." Ronald E. Purser, Professor of Management, San Francisco State University, and author of *Time and Temporality in the Network Society*

"A stunning book. A paradigm breaking insight into the essence of work, organization, and enrichment (both financial & spiritual). It's a tough read with huge pots of gold along the way. The book is our age's version of *The Structure of Scientific Revolution* applied to business. It's a revolution and an evolution." Martin Rutte, Founder & Chair of the Board,

"This fascinating new book, combining the author's deep spiritual understanding with a lifetime's experience in business and management, provides a unique analysis of modern management practices." Professor Jacqueline C. Vischer, Faculty of Environmental Design and Director of the New Work Environments Research Group, University of Montreal

"Since first reading Albert Low's book, *Zen and Creative Management*, I have used / referred to this book in my graduate management courses as a description of how to see management in a more holistic perspective. I look forward to incorporating insights from his new book, *Conflict and Creativity at Work*, into my management classes." Rexford H. Draman, Associate Professor, School of Business, University of Texas at Brownsville

"*Conflict and Creativity at Work* is a must read for all managers and concerned citizens who want to understand why tyranny and power now dominate corporate America. Albert Low goes beyond the myths of corporate capitalism and journalistic accounts of corporate greed to help us better understand our personal roles and responsibilities as managers and citizens. He is not just writing about business ethics but about what makes us human and by doing so he confronts our vulnerabilities while providing vision and hope for a sustainable world." Terry Armstrong, Organizational Consultant

"Whatever your profession this book allows you to view the workplace as an extension of your mind. Creative minds have fun making conflicts less frightening: Albert Low brings you a fresh and persuasive guide." José Prieto, Professor of Personnel Psychology, University of Madrid

"Albert Low persuasively reveals the hidden dimensions of organizations, diving deep into the recesses of human nature. He points out the dynamic tension between two seemingly incompatible frames of reference — namely, the dynamics of striving for dynamic unity while expressing individuality. Low provides a provocative way of humanizing organizations, emphasizing the importance of process and attention to human needs over profits and the maximizing of shareholder wealth. Drawing examples from Zen and other religions, Low argues that spirituality and creativity in organizations will come from a change in the way people and organizations think. This ground-breaking book will be a valuable addition to the business school curriculum." Jerry Biberman, University of Scanton, Co-Editor of the *Journal of Management, Spirituality and Religion*

Dedicated to the memory of
Elliott Jaques

CONFLICT
and CREATIVITY
at WORK

Human Roots of Corporate Life

ALBERT LOW

sussex
ACADEMIC
PRESS
BRIGHTON • PORTLAND

2 4 6 8 10 9 7 5 3

First published 2008 in Great Britain by
SUSSEX ACADEMIC PRESS
PO Box 139
Eastbourne BN24 9BP

and in the United States of America by
SUSSEX ACADEMIC PRESS
920 NE 58th Ave   Suite 300
Portland, Oregon 97213-3786

British Library Cataloguing in Publication Data
A CIP catalogue record for this book is available from the British Library.

Library of Congress Cataloging-in-Publication Data
Low, Albert.
Creativity and conflict at work : human roots of corporate
life / Albert Low.
p. cm.
Includes bibliographical references and index.
ISBN 978-1-84519-272-3 (p/b : alk. paper)
1. Work. 2. Creative ability. 3. Corporations. 4. Quality
of work life. 5. Social responsibility of business. I. Title.
BF481.L69 2008
302.3'5—dc22

2008010870

Mixed Sources
Product group from well-managed
forests and other controlled sources
www.fsc.org Cert no. SGS-COC-2482
© 1996 Forest Stewardship Council

Typeset and designed by SAP, Brighton & Eastbourne
Printed by TJ International, Padstow, Cornwall.
This book is printed on acid-free paper.

Contents

Foreword by
Alfonso Montuori

I was browsing in a Bangkok bookstore in February of 1986 when to my great surprise I found a little volume called *Zen and Creative Management*. At the time I was teaching graduate management students at Central-South University in Hunan, China. The supply of interesting and relevant reading material was limited to what I had brought with me. This was the era when *In Pursuit of Excellence* and *The Art of Japanese Management* were considered leading edge, and the university library's management section seemed to specialize mostly in Accounting. I needed something more stimulating. Briefly escaping the bitter cold of Central China for the steamy heat of Thailand, I had come across an unexpected treasure. This wasn't just leading edge — it seemed to originate in an entirely different world. When, many years later, I finally had the pleasure of meeting the author in person and showed him my copy, it was embarrassingly tattered from 20 years of constant use and held together mostly with scotch tape. Fortunately I had bought several other copies since, in case my original one simply turned to dust.

Zen and Creative Management was Albert Low's first book. Published in 1976, it was enormously exciting and innovative. Twenty years later it had sold 75,000 copies. *Fast Company* magazine featured it, and pointed out how ahead of his time Low had been — and continues to be. His approach was and is ruthlessly original. His inquiry was clearly not guided by the flavor of the month management trend, by the confines of academic management discourse, or the tunnel vision that all too often comes from a mono-cultural, mono-disciplinary perspective. Low grounded his work in his own extensive experience as a manager, and drew, among others, on the razor sharp insights of iconoclastic management theorist Elliott Jaques, the innovative systemic thinking of the British mystic J. G. Bennett, the ethology of Robert Ardrey, the creativity research of novelist and freethinker Arthur Koestler, and to cap it all, Zen theory and practice. Throughout the book, Low was proposing a radically different way of thinking about management. But he was also proposing a radically different worldview.

Conflict and *Creativity at Work* takes up where *Zen and Creative Management* left off. It revisits many of the same themes, and rightly so: they are at the core of the experience of work, management, and organization. After more than 30 years, numerous important books under his belt, and continually deepening his Zen practice (Low is now a teacher at the Montreal Zen Center and a highly regarded figure in the Zen tradition), we find a book that benefits from a more fully worked out philosophical perspective. The words "philosophical perspective" may raise concerns in readers not accustomed to seeing the words *philosophical* and *management* together. And yet a philosophical reconsideration of management is precisely what is needed in a time of crisis and transition such as ours.

A common criticism of the popular management literature is that it rarely offers anything new. Much of it is old wine in new bottles. It is not particularly inspiring, innovative or interesting. Sadly, it's also often not particularly useful. Perhaps one of the reasons why a good portion of the management literature has been so uninspiring is that it has simply not been radical enough. It has not questioned the fundamental assumptions of management deeply enough. And given the enormous transformation occurring in the world economy, the shift in many countries to a "post-materialist" society, and the mind-boggling complexity, speed, and ambiguity of the work environment, it is undoubtedly essential to question fundamental assumptions. The point that the world is changing has been made often — talk of a "paradigm shift" abounds. While much of the literature gets to the edge, it never presents satisfying alternatives.

Low has approached the topic with deep experience, and the insight he brings as a former manager, a scholar, and a Zen master. He is not selling anything, and has no investment in the world that normally generates works on this subject. This is partly what gives this book its tremendous freshness, its unusual perspective. Low also realizes that in order to achieve a true change, he cannot be limited by the discourse of management. Hence his extended and important forays into perception, ambiguity, logic, and the nature of thinking. Without them, he would not be able to create the capacious framework that allows for a rethinking of both management theory and practice.

Conflict and Creativity at Work starts with a profound and stunning premise: Creativity is not some terribly unusual gift bestowed on selected individuals, but rather the very nature and condition of human existence, and, specifically for this book, of work. Low takes this fundamental premise and explores its relevance for management and organizations, inviting us to challenge and overthrow some cherished assumptions. Taking us on a tour of human perception, thinking, and organization, we find that after reading him we have a much broader and spacious understanding of the issues, and may be inclined to act differently.

Particularly rewarding about this work is its deeply *radical* nature. Radical in the sense of pertaining to the most basic aspects of a phenomenon, its roots, and also — following the dictionary definition — far-reaching, thoroughgoing, and making sweeping changes. Along with the "radical" step of taking creativity as a "frame" through which to understand life, thought, work, and organization, Low also adds a very important set of definitions. Low is literally radical by going to these key terms and challenging us to look at what they mean, how we use them, and what an appropriate, workable definition might be. What is a corporation? What is work? What is a product? We use these terms every day, but in many ways it's not at all clear what they mean or how they are being used. Low cites the case of Harvard business school professor Joseph Badaracco who admitted that in 25 years of teaching he had never been asked what a corporation is. And yet management carries with it the aura of "science," a hangover from the days of Frederick Taylor, but also playing in to the present obsession with "metrics."

An example of Low's profoundly radical approach is his definition of a "product." What's so good or interesting about a definition of a product, you might ask? We all know what a product is. Or at least we think we do. The business of business is, besides business, as Milton Friedman put it (a definition Low criticizes quite sharply) is *products* — whatever they are. Low defines a product as "an idea, in a form, with a demand." At first glance this might seem almost trivial. But if we look at the implications and ramifications, we'll see that Low's concise definition of a product is very *generative*. It opens up a world of possibilities, and makes us see the everyday as if for the first time. It doesn't just connect the concept of product to creativity, but also to work and to a systemic, contextual way of thinking.

Conflict and Creativity at Work deserves a very close reading. The ideas presented are quite revolutionary. They certainly cannot be absorbed with a quick skim. In other words, this is not an ordinary management book, but a book to be read, re-read, savored and explored in great depth. It is designed to provide us with a completely different way of seeing creativity, work, management and organizations. No small feat. It is provocative and often brilliant. In an age of sound bites, catchy slogans, and institutionalized, mediated attention deficit disorder it may seem a daunting task to immerse oneself in a dense book that in some ways turns a lot of our fundamental assumptions on their head. Kurt Lewin famously stated that there's nothing as useful as a good theory. *Conflict and Creativity at Work* is a perfect example.

Alfonso Montuori, Ph.D.
Department Chair,
Professor Transformative Leadership
Transformative Studies
California Institute of Integral Studies
San Francisco

Preface and Acknowledgments

Conflict and Creativity at Work: the human roots of corporate life started life as an update of *Zen and Creative Management* that went out of print in 2003 after a long and successful career. I began writing *Zen and Creative Management* in 1963 and finished it in 1974. It was published by three different publishing houses — Anchor Books, Playboy Press, and Charles E. Tuttle — and sold about 75,000 copies. A number of universities have used it in courses on management. Notable among these are the University of California, the California Institute of Integral Studies, the University of Madrid, and St Edwards University's School of Management and Business, Texas; many people, university professors among them, urged me to bring the book up to date.

However, I soon realized after I started the revision that I would have to rewrite the book entirely in order to take account of changes in the business world. Although it is widely accepted that we live in the age of information I feel this way of thinking puts the emphasis in the wrong place. Our age is now the age of ideas and, more than ever, the main requirement in industry and commerce is not so much the processing and transmission of information as the nurturing of creativity and the development of ideas. This requirement is the central theme of *Conflict and Creativity at Work*. In addition, the corruption and lack of corporate responsibility that occurred during the eighties and nineties in some corporations, and recognition of the damage that our heedless use of resources has done to the environment, compels us all to question the very basis on which our industrial society has been built.

Zen and Creative Management pointed out the main defect in the corporate structure: the widespread assumption that a company operates simply in the interests of its stockholders. This defect has undoubtedly contributed greatly to the difficulties of pollution, corporate governance and resource depletion that western countries are currently facing. *Zen and Creative Management* also emphasized the importance that ideas have in the corporate world. But I felt that these two problems — to give a realistic diagnosis of the ills of corporate life and to provide an environment conducive to creativity — interwoven as they are, should become the main themes of this current book.

The world faces a crisis at the present time. Band-aids and patchwork technical solutions will not be enough to get us through it. Al Gore's *An Inconvenient Truth* can surely leave us in no doubt about the scale of the problem. But a crisis is also a great opportunity. If we can think boldly and creatively about the dilemmas that we all face, a new society can be created, a society in which *human beings are the central concern.* This book is written in the hope that it will make a worthwhile contribution to the birth of a new society, better equipped to face the challenges ahead.

I would like to acknowledge the help that I received from the following people while writing this book.

My gratitude goes to my wife Jean for her help, encouragement and skilful editing, to Alfonso Montuori for his constant encouragement and suggestions, to Jaqueline Vischer, Roger Brouillette, Pierre Lanoix and my son John, who read and made valuable comments for improving the manuscript.

There is a widespread, almost universal, under estimation
of the impact of organization on how we go about our
business . . . Creativity and innovation, like freedom
and liberty, depend not upon the soft pedaling
of organization, but upon the development
of institutions with the kind of constraints
and opportunities that can enable us to
live and work together harmoniously.

Elliott Jaques, *Requisite Management*
(Arlington: Cason Hall, 1996), p. 10.

Stockholder privilege rests on the notion that corporations
are not human communities but pieces of property,
which mean they can be owned and sold by
the properties class.

Marjorie Kelly, *The Divine Right of Capital*
(San Francisco: Berrett-Koehler, 2003).

Introduction

The famous question, "Is man made for the Sabbath or is the Sabbath made for man?" has its modern counterpart: is the corporate system made for human beings or are human beings made for the corporate system? The question is becoming ever more relevant. During the past twenty-five years our confidence in the system has been badly shaken. The ravages of corporate greed have ripped through the fabric of society like a tornado, leaving gashes that perhaps cannot be mended. Trust is one of the most valuable of our non-renewable resources. When it becomes polluted and we can no longer trust, only tyranny and power can replace it as the means for sustaining the society in which we live. Enron, WorldCom, the tainted attempt at the leveraged buy out of RJR Nabisco, the price fixing that was revealed through the ADM scandal,[1] the Dot com. bubble that burst, the 'Gomery' scandals in Canada, Conrad Black — the list just goes on.

Who benefits from all this corruption? The stockholders? But they now have to sue companies that have misused their investments. The customers? Not if prices are fixed and the customers manipulated in a multitude of ways by these corporations. The employees? "In the last decade and a half the proportion of employees making *poverty-level wages* has climbed substantially, and in mid 1990's it stood at an alarming 30 percent"[2] (emphasis added). So the question remains: who is it all for?

The myth of course is that a corporation is made by and for the stockholders, and that they own it. Yet most of the money invested by stockholders does not go to corporations but to other speculators. Indeed, during the last thirty years very few of the Dow Jones Industrials have sold any common stock. "According to figures from the Federal Reserve in recent years only one in a hundred dollars trading on the public markets has been reaching corporations."[3]

The stock market has become more a place for gambling than a place for solid investment. Gambling is an addiction. Compound that addiction with the addiction to power, and an unholy alliance is formed. Ken

Auletta writing in his book *Greed and Glory on Wall Street: The fall of the house of Lehman* surmises that "Human folly and foibles — not the bottom line of profits, not business acumen, not 'scientific management' or the perfect marketing plans or execution — often determine the success or failure of an organization."[4]

To dub insatiable greed and lust for power 'follies' and 'foibles' hardly does them justice. Ninety percent of the financial wealth in the United States is owned by only 10 percent of the population, and the one percent wealthiest doubled their share of national household wealth during the last twenty years from 20 percent to close to 40 percent.[5] Yet still, among the 10 percent are those who break the law and indulge in corrupt practices to increase their portion even further.

Social activists are drawing attention to the damage being done to the environment, to the exploitation of the poor in third world countries, to the waste of diminishing resources, to pollution, global warming and to many other concerns. They are pressing for government controls and regulations. Even some shareholders and shareholder groups are now actively trying to reduce the damage being done to society by the companies in which their money is supposedly invested. Furthermore, courses on ethics and corporate social responsibility are now given in universities and business schools. Yet much is based on a faulty assumption: that executives, within the present corporate system, can do things differently. Sam Gibara, Chairman and former CEO of Goodyear Tire said, "Although the perception is that you have absolute power to do whatever you want, the reality is that you do not have that power. As a person you may want to act one way, but as a CEO you cannot do that."[6]

Foibles and follies do not drive the system, and greed is not the cause but the result of the system. Let me quote Marjorie Kelly once more: "The prime force [that drives the corporate system] is *systemic pressure, pressure that comes from the design of the system itself.*[7] The pressure to 'get the numbers' (generate profits for shareholders) is felt by CEOs or managers — and enforced by them — but it originates with the financial interests behind corporations" (my emphasis).[8] And those financial interests are succored by a myth, the myth that a company functions simply in the interests of the stockholder. Thus the corporate system functions to promote and maintain the corporate system. Human beings simply serve it, and where possible, exploit it. Is the corporate system not the dreaded Frankenstein Monster that Mary Wollstonecraft Shelley warned us about so long ago?

Let us return to the roots

If real changes are to be made, involving real corporate social responsibility and higher ethical standards, the system must be re-examined from a different perspective. As long as corporations stay within the present mythical perspective — that the needs of the stockholder take natural precedence over all other needs — they will simply remain within the limits imposed by that perspective, and the best they can hope for are band-aids where major surgery may be needed. But how can they break free of these limits? Where can they look to find an understanding or explanation of corporate behavior that is not already biased by the existing perspective? Business schools and universities cannot provide the answers. They are, for the most part, the purveyors of the myth. Schools and universities cannot give a securely founded understanding of the origin of the corporation.

Some people may well object to the idea that business schools cannot provide answers. But take for example the word 'company'. One uses the word often — one may work for a company, possibly invest in a company, and no doubt one is a customer of many companies. Nobel Prize winner Milton Friedman says that a company is 'an artificial legal structure'. But the articles of incorporation, the letters patent and so on are not really the company; they simply make a company possible. Is a company then its buildings or land? A company can change its premises and nevertheless be the 'same' company. Is it the people who are investing in the company? All the shares? The employees? What does the word company refer to?

Do business schools teach the meaning of the word 'company'? Joe Badaracco, Harvard Professor of Business Ethics, admitted that in his twenty-five years of teaching he had never been asked that question![9] Webster's Dictionary states that a company is "an association of persons for carrying on a commercial or industrial enterprise." That might give us a start, although it does not say what kind of association these persons have, or account for the role of money in a company, nor does it mention work, which after all is a vital requirement if the company is to survive. For the Web a company is "in general, any group of persons united to pursue a common interest", or "an institution created to conduct business." The equivalent in physics of these definitions would be to define an atom as a number of things brought together. They are hardly good enough to form a secure foundation for an understanding of the corporate system on which to build a system of ethics, a system for which many are searching.

Work is the most essential ingredient in a company yet the word 'work' is another that one uses frequently, takes for granted that all under-stand it in the same way, but is hard put to say what it means. One goes to work, does work, is paid for work, but what is work? What does the word 'work' mean? Something hard, activity one is paid to do, the expen-diture of energy?

Yet another vague word is profit. What does the word 'profit' mean? Is the purpose of a company simply to make a profit and, if so, for whom? What is 'profit'? Hardly the bottom-line because the bottom line is more often than not simply the result of some accounting wizardry. All these questions are interconnected: to answer one in some way implies an answer to them all. A viable and fact based theory of a company will have to define these terms and show their interconnection.

Elliott Jaques in his book *Requisite Organization* is one of the few people who have seriously questioned the meaning of the words used in the corporate world. He says, "There *is not one single unequivocally defined concept in the whole field.*"[10] He lists twelve of the most commonly used words in a manager's lexicon, including 'manager', 'supervisor', 'responsibility', 'performance', 'authority', 'CEO', and 'organization'. Any rational discussion, or worthwhile understanding, must be based on clearly defined concepts. But, as he says, "Lack of clarity is the ruling state of affairs in organizations and the field of management science." At the moment such questions as "Is the corpo-rate system made for human beings or are human beings made for the corporate system?" or, "In whose name is corporate activity being done?" cannot be thought about intelligently. This is so because even the meaning of the expression 'corporate system' remains unknown.

Creativity as the root

I am going to suggest that the key to gaining understanding of the terms 'work', 'corporation', 'profit', 'company growth' and many others, and to grasping the prime motivating force of entrepreneurial, managerial and investment capitalism, is 'creativity' — what it means to be a creative person, and what the connection is between creativity and work.

Human beings are naturally creative. Seizing hold of this truth as the root and source of corporate human behavior will enable us to build a foundation for understanding and organizing a company that enhances, and does not inhibit, creativity, work and correct decision making. Such a foundation will be firmly embedded in the bedrock of human nature, and will replace the current myth that panders to our greed, and that is based upon faulty assumptions.

A company is an extension of the human mind

A company organization is not simply a creation of the human mind; it is *an extension* of the human mind. To be more specific, the mind of a manager and a company organization are, to some extent, *isomorphic*. Because I will use the word 'isomorphic' frequently let us be quite sure that we understand the word in the same way. Isomorphic means 'the same shape'. (*Iso* means the 'same' and *morphic* means 'shape'.) A camera and an eye are, to some extent, isomorphic; so are the lens of a magnifying glass and the lens of an eye; and so are a backhoe and an arm and hand. Just as a telescope is an extension of a person's eye, so the organization of a company is an extension of a manager's mind. Therefore, if human beings are naturally creative, a company too is naturally creative, provided it is organized appropriately.

As an extension of the human mind a company is also a pseudo-organism. One of the chief characteristics of an organism is that it can make copies of itself. A company grows by a process of self-replication. In a one-person business, work may increase to the point that the person cannot do it all himself. So he employs and trains another to do the work. The job has copied itself. In a similar way, a company can replicate itself by setting up branches in different locations. Moreover, a company has the potential for growth, expansion and self-regulation, which are also characteristics of an organism. An organism takes in food from the environment and transforms it into action. The human organisms also transforms impressions into ideas. A company does likewise, its food being raw materials and components, knowledge and information.

What I have said so far fits in with the legal understanding that a company, or rather a corporation, "is a legal entity (distinct from a natural person) that often has similar rights in law to those of a natural person."[11] As a 'person' a company can buy and sell property, borrow money, sue and be sued. I am now suggesting that as a pseudo-organism it can think and create. It can also go mad. Although one can subject a mind to a certain amount of stress, the amount is limited. In the same way an organization can only suffer so much abuse before it too begins to show signs of breaking down. The mind suffers stress when one of its parts is at odds with other parts. I will show that an organization too will similarly suffer stress when parts are opposed to other parts. The film *The Corporation* went so far as to say that the modern company is psychopathic and used the psychiatric determinants of psychopathology to make its point.

One of the contributors to *The Corporation*, Ray Anderson, is the CEO of the world's largest carpet manufacturer. He too is concerned that the corporate system is not based on any real understanding. He used rather a dramatic way to make his point. The film showed the early attempts that men made to fly. The last attempt in the film showed a plane being pushed off the edge of a cliff and going into free fall. Anderson said that the pilot might think that the plane was flying but, because it was not built according to the laws of aero-dynamics, the plane must inevitably crash. He was pointing out that because the corporation has deviated so far from its roots — the laws of human nature — it too is in free-fall and, unless something is done to bring it more in line with those roots, it too must crash.

An outline of the book

The corporate system is a product of human creativity. This book elaborates on the meaning and consequences of that statement. It shows an entirely new way to think about a corporation, and shows how ethical standards and corporate social responsibility naturally arise out of the new understanding thus provided.

To understand a company, its organization and its reason for being, we must understand:

1 Why, and in what way, human beings are naturally creative, and the connection that creativity has with conflict.
2 How creativity and conflict are expressed in work, and why work is necessary for our mental health.
3 How the corporate system has emerged out of human creativity.
4 How the company organization can promote creativity through the judicious use of conflict.
5 What is meant by the expression 'an ethical corporation'.

Structure of the book

The book is divided into an Introduction and five parts.

The Introduction *tells why another theory of management is needed.*

Part One, *The Dynamics of Human Nature*, is concerned with the first questions:
Why are human beings naturally creative, and what connection does creativity have with conflict?

When considering a company and its organization, human creativity is the most important feature that we must bear in mind. Furthermore, creativity and work share a common *dynamic* structure. In other words creativity, work, and the company that grows out of them, are ongoing. Every situation is different: *a company does not change; a company is change.* An 'entity' called a company that is subject to inner and outer influences does not exist.

In Part One, therefore, I show what I mean by 'creativity' and how creativity grows out of perception. I then show the connection between creativity, work and conflict. Furthermore, the way we currently think often restricts, and sometimes even inhibits our creativity. Our present way of thinking is based on the belief that in order to solve a problem it must be broken into its component parts, and then each part dealt with separately. Such a reductive way of thinking is called either *analytical* thinking or *logical* thinking, which is a legitimate way, but only if balanced and complemented by a thinking that involves the whole situation beyond its parts. So I develop a new way of thinking that involves *ambiguity* and that includes, but goes beyond, logical thinking, and, in turn, will lead to a new way of thinking about an organization. Such will be the chief contribution of the book. *Unless we know how to think correctly about a company we shall organize in an ad hoc way, a way that can cause endless confusion.*

I will not say how to organize a company; I have no *Six Easy Steps to Better Management* to offer. It has been said that to help someone who is in need you do not give him a fish: you give him a fishing rod. To give *Six Easy Steps to Better Management* or something similar is to give a fish; to show how to think realistically about a company and its organization is to give the fishing rod.

Part Two, *The Origins of Stress*, is concerned with the questions: *How is human creativity expressed in work, and why is work necessary for our mental health?*

I define the word *work* and show the importance work has in the ecology of being, then show why work is hard. The job of filing assistant is given as the simplest example of work. Work must have limits and these limits become more complex as one ascends the management hiearchy. Limits are the result of *dilemmas* such as Structure/Process, System/Individual, Urgent/Important, among others.

I then describe in detail two jobs in a company according to the dilemmas with which they have to contend in order to show the basic structure of the dilemmas underlying all jobs.

In place of 'management by objectives' I suggest an alternative:

management by product. A product is an *idea in a form with a demand*.
I discuss the meaning and power of an idea as well as the fact that the
form of a product is not always material, then examine 'the idea' within
the context of the basic dilemma.

Part Three, *The Company Field*, is concerned with the question:
How has the corporate system emerged out of human creativity?

Part Three describes the structure of the company and the relation
that it has to all that I have said about creativity, work and conflict. I
define a company as *a multidimensional field of commitment, capable
of growth, expansion, and self-regulation, having the contradictory drives
to survive and to fulfill its mission, with a product as its dynamic center.*
Part Three begins by amplifying the definition; then shows the field to be
under tension and shows further why creative tension and conflict are
necessary.

Part Four, *Conflict, Creativity and Capacity*, deals with the questions:
*How can the company organization promote creativity through the
judicious use of conflict?*

*What qualities does an employee need to have to do the work
assigned?*

Three kinds of conflict arise in a company: two are non-productive,
the third is productive and arises out of the creative tension of the field.
Territoriality can cause non-productive conflict and I discuss territoriality
at length.
Higher levels of work emerge as a company grows, and these levels
require correspondingly higher levels of capacity and ability. I examine
the meaning of commitment and its accompanying needs, and then
show the nature of capacity and ability.

Part Five, *Ownership and Ethics*, brings together some of the main
themes of the book to show the way that genuine spirituality and reliable ethical standards can be introduced into a company.
I raise the question, "Who owns the company?" and show the ramifications of such a question in the light of all that has been said
in the book. Finally, I show how legitimate ethical standards and
authentic spirituality can become natural attributes of a well-organized
company.

Notes

1 "It has become apparent that price-fixing was a workaday endeavor around the globe, involving scores of corporations." Kurt Eichenwald, *The Informant* (New York: Broadway Books, 2000), p. 559.
2 Marjorie Kelly, *The Divine Right of Capital*, p. 26.
3 *Ibid.*, p. 20.
4 Ken Auletta, *Greed and Glory on Wall Street: The fall of the house of Lehman* (Woodstock and New York: The Overlook Press, 2001).
5 Kelly, *The Divine Right of Capital*, p. xiv.
6 The film *The Corporation.*
7 Kelly, *The Divine Right of Capital*, p. 52.
8 *Ibid.*
9 *Ibid.*
10 Jaques, *Requisite Management*, p.10.
11 Definition taken from the Web: <http://www.google.com/search?hl=en&client=safari&rls=en&defl=en&q=define:corporation&sa=X&oi=glossary_definition&ct=title>.

PART ONE

The Dynamics of
Human Nature

CHAPTER ONE

The Origins of Stress

The importance of understanding ourselves

To understand why we do the things that we do in life — why we work, why work is organized the way it is, what creativity is and why creativity is so important — we must first understand ourselves. What are we? Quite obviously an organization cannot exist without people, and yet this is so often overlooked. Even though organizations must be designed with people in mind, all too often managers who have to organize a department simply think about goals or objectives, about cost reduction or about specific kinds of work that must be done, about principles of organization, or, worse still, about different ways of drawing organization charts. As Joel Bakan says in his book, *The Corporation*,[1] "The company and its underlying ideology are animated by a narrow conception of human nature that is too distorted and too uninspiring to have lasting purchase on our political imagination."

That work is a natural out-come of the way human beings have evolved, and that therefore the problem is how to channel work in such a way that it is not wasted, is not generally taken into account. Of course many writers have said that we work for other reasons than simply that of earning a living. But, as Maria Callas is reputed to have said, "I work therefore I am." To understand the dynamics of organization the dynamics of what we are must be understood, at least to the extent of being able to see that the one flows naturally out of the other. This does not mean that a manager must be a psychologist. He is not required to manipulate or tamper with the psychic make-up of people who work for him, or to use psychology to manipulate, motivate and control them. But he must know enough about human nature to know what can and cannot be done.

Basically very little needs to be known, but that very little is difficult to know because generally most people have never really bothered to enquire about what motivates us, why we suffer, why we fall in love or why we work, and so have no basis on which to build an understanding. To understand others we must first understand ourselves, and this can be a long and painful task. Perhaps a year or two devoted to this, rather than spending those years at university reading about the thoughts and opinions of others, might be time well spent.

Those who have enquired into the human mind, including those who have written about leadership, about motivation, and about why people work, have almost always made their enquiries from outside, studying other people rather than first studying themselves. This approach means that they so often live on the surface of their lives, and their understanding is equally superficial. Elliott Jaques, who was both a psychoanalyst and a management consultant and theorist, points out that this superficiality has led to a restless flow of wasteful and futile fads and panaceas. Overcoming this problem of superficiality, he goes on to say, "requires not slogans and gimmicks but the development of a thorough going understanding of the nature of the organizations we use to get our work done."[2]

Because I am not going to stay within the context of academic psychological theory, or the theories of business taught at business schools, much of what follows about human nature, work and its organization will be novel, surprising and perhaps difficult to accept. Furthermore, because much is novel or has been put in a novel context, it will take a while to develop; but at the end of the journey I am confident that you will have found the time well spent, and will have a new basis for thinking about work and its importance to human life. With such a way of thinking we can start to reexamine the old myths and replace them with an understanding founded on solid facts.

On stress and creativity

Most of us are familiar with tension, anxiety, anger and the feeling at times of being in conflict with life. We are also familiar with the feeling that work is hard, even though we may like the work that we do. Furthermore, human beings are essentially creative. This chapter will be a discussion of human creativity, as well as a discussion of why we find work hard, and why life is so often difficult and painful — an essential preamble to defining creativity, and to showing that the most important aspect of work is its creative aspect.

Our stress, anxiety depression and other negative states are often looked upon as pathological, as states that have to be 'cured'. The most widely held psychological theory is that negative mind states arise because of traumas, or at least major difficulties that occurred in the past, probably due to some fault in our upbringing.

A different way of looking at stress is to see that human life itself is stressful.[3] Furthermore, the cause of stress lies upstream of the conscious mind. Psychological traumas and difficulties do not cause suffering; they release it. They act like the trigger of a gun. The trigger does not cause the explosion that sends the bullet on its way; it releases it. Stress, moreover, is not just negative and undesirable; stress and conflict are essential elements in the creative process.

I shall start by developing the notion that although we are all individuals, we are at the same time divided within ourselves, in conflict with ourselves at the very heart of our being. This notion will provide an understanding of why life is stressful, and why so often an underlying sense of malaise or anxiety pervades our life. It will also lay the foundation for understanding creativity and work.

On individuality

Each person is an individual and the word 'individual' means indivisible. *Individuus* is the Latin equivalent of the Greek word *atom*. Most people see themselves as one, as a unity, as a single person. Moreover, we are restless and active during most of our lives: if not physically, then mentally. Many feel driven, feeling the need to 'get somewhere'. When we are blocked and frustrated the feeling of 'not getting anywhere' surges up, of 'life going nowhere'. Our life is filled with intentions, aims, hopes and goals. So we are not only one, but at the same time a dynamic, intentional and purposeful one.

Dynamic, purposeful unity was, at one time, called *will*, a word that was replaced in psychological literature by the word *conation*, but both words have now become somewhat old-fashioned. Nowadays the word *unconscious* tends to be used in place of will. If I asked you, "How do you come to a decision?" "How do you drive a car?" or even "How do you stand up?" you would probably say, "I don't know. I just do it. Its unconscious." The tendency to use the word 'unconscious' has come from the pervasive influence of Freudian psychoanalysis, which only recently has begun to be discredited as a scientific account of how and why we act as we do. But, even though discredited, many of Freud's ideas have become deeply embedded in Western culture, and the notion of the unconscious is probably the most important of these.

The conscious mind plays a very small part in most of our activity.[4] You can easily verify this. When you speak, for example, you do not know the words that you are going to use before you say them; when you stand, you do not know what muscles to use. Yet the words do not come out in a random fashion, but in the way that you intended; when you get up from a chair you use just the right amount of energy. If these are not conscious acts, although admittedly consciousness may accompany them, then the tendency to say that they must be unconscious seems natural.

The problem with the word 'unconscious' is that it implies that the source of all action is somehow less than consciousness; that this source is in some way deficient. This was another of Freud's ideas: he believed that as much as possible must be rescued from a primitive and infantile unconscious and brought into consciousness, must be raised from darkness into light. Yet other traditions, for example the Buddhist, believe that the conscious mind is the deficient mind, that the rational intellect is a limitation on a much greater, more creative and spontaneous mind. Thus consciousness could be likened to a filter through which shines the light of will. I shall be looking at consciousness in this way.

It can be said that a transcendent dynamism, a drive towards unity, transcends the conscious mind, and releases a restless need for action. It is transcendent because it is upstream of, or transcends, consciousness. I will call it simply *dynamic unity* although words like 'intention', 'commitment', 'application', 'dedication', and 'devotion' will be used when dynamic unity is filtered through consciousness. Dynamic unity, as commitment, is a vital aspect of work, creativity and organization. Indeed, it makes these both possible and necessary.

The universe is one

Because of dynamic unity you know yourself to be an individual; so, in the same way, because of dynamic unity you know the universe to be One. The word 'universe' means 'turning to the one'. Dynamic unity is all-pervasive. Indeed it could be looked upon as a cosmic imperative: *Let there be One!* that not only causes us to see the universe as one, but also has us see, paradoxically, that every 'thing' in the universe is one also. A Greek philosopher, Plotinus, put the matter succinctly when he said, "It is by the One that all beings are beings. (If) not a one, a thing is not. No army, no choir, no flock exists except that it be one. No house, even, or ship exists except as the one."[5] In other words, wherever you look you see one. The French language insists upon this one because, instead of saying 'a' table, 'a' desk 'a' chair, the French say 'une' table, 'un' bureau, 'une' chaise. The 'une' or 'un' can be translated either as 'a' or 'one'. The tendency to see 'ones', *gestalts* or wholes, is an important element in creativity and work.

That everything is one is taken for granted. It is so evident, so obvious and unchanging that we overlook its significance. Because it is so obvious and taken for granted it can easily be ignored and seen to be of no account. However, a group of psychologists in the middle of the last century saw it as a most important principle of the human mind. They came to be called *Gestalt psychologists*. They insisted that the whole, or the one, is a basic principle in both perception and in activity. Not only have the *Gestalt* psychologists shown the importance of the one; the artist, the architect, the musician, mystic, scientist, dancer, mathematician all in their own way reveal the importance of unity, which they may sometimes call truth, or beauty, good or holy. Unity is a prime force in work and creativity; it is also a prime force in the creation of a company.

One but two

The drama of life arises because we are not only one, we are also two: in the very core of our being we are divided against ourselves. From this division comes the feeling, 'I am here, you are there', 'I am here, the world is there'; a duality that is taken quite for granted. Language insists on such a duality — a complete sentence must have a subject and an object. The way we think also constantly divides the world — it is either one thing or the other; it is either this or that. Later I will show how widespread dichotomies are in corporate life. A dualistic view of the world leads to dilemmas and ambiguities that often cause much unnecessary frustration and difficulty. The profound sense of separateness and alienation from which many people suffer comes from our being divided against ourselves. That these dichotomies come from the way we are, and so from the way we view the world and not from the way that the world is, escapes us.

Because we are one but two, the source of activity, creativity and work, our ambition and efforts to get ahead, comes not from dynamic unity but from the drive to rediscover lost unity, and so avoid the pain that being divided against ourselves causes. This drive is expressed in the myths of the Holy Grail, the crock at the end of the rainbow, the Promised Land, the alchemists' Philosopher's Stone, even in Melville's novel, Moby Dick. The philosopher Plato said that romantic love is the "burning longing for this unity." According to him we have a burning longing because the Gods separated us from ourselves.

Both Buddhism and Christianity have explanations for our wounded state, and the explanations are very similar. According to Christian teaching the wound was inflicted when Adam and Eve disobeyed God and ate the fruit of the tree of knowledge of good and evil. In other words, they turned their back on unity as their source and entered the world of dichotomies and dualities of good and evil, of right and wrong, life and death. And so life, according to the Catholic tradition, is pervaded by the consequences of Original Sin, which the medieval theologians said, "wounded us in our natural way of acting."[6]

Just as Christian teaching says we are wounded because Adam and Eve, and subsequently humanity, turned their backs on their source, so Buddhist teaching says that we inflict the wound on ourselves by ignoring, or turning our back on our source. Ignorance is the primary sin in Buddhism and is the reason that life is suffering. The Sanskrit word for 'suffering' is *duhkha*, which also means duality. These myths tell us that because division, conflict, and suffering pervade all experience they are not learnt, and cannot have been derived from experience. Indeed division makes experience necessary. We seek relief from the pain of conflict by seeking a stable point of reference, a dynamic center, and conscious experience is centered on this stable point.

The story of Narcissus, the young man who saw himself reflected in a pool and fell in love with himself, also contains hints of a divided state, a state in which the self reflects itself. We talk about self-awareness and self-consciousness, which are after all the self reflecting the self. Awareness of awareness is generally looked upon as the precursor to consciousness. The words 'disgust',[7] 'distract', and 'distraught', indeed many of the words beginning with 'dis'— meaning two — point to our divided state. The way we sometimes speak in times of stress also point to a division, a schism, and of the problems that it causes. We say, "I was beside myself with fear, or anger, or remorse;" or "I fell apart," or "I was in two minds," or "I jumped out of my skin."

One of the more interesting aspects of the split is the tendency that many of us have to talk to ourselves, usually sub-vocally. People who follow a form of spiritual work that includes staying present at all times, find that an incessant mono-dialogue goes on in their minds. If I am talking to myself, am I two, the one that is talking as well as the one that is being talked to, or just one, just me?

If you observe someone that you know well you will find that they may have two quite different personalities. One will be compliant, pleasant, somewhat laid back; the other may be domineering, ambitious, restless and difficult to get along with. Luis Buñuel, the Spanish film director, built the film *Cet obscure objet du désir* around the duality of a personality. Two quite different actresses played the part of Conchita, the chief character of the film. One played a compliant, seductive Conchita; the other played a bad tempered and cold Conchita.

Someone who believes that the brain is the main, or even the only determinant of behavior will have a ready explanation for all that has been said about the two ways of being. As is now well known, the brain has two sides and it seems that, by and large, the left side controls analytical functions and the right controls intuitive functions. But this is not the place to enter into a discussion about the relative merits of the brain versus a more spiritual interpretation. We do not need to know the origin of the split; it is enough for us to realize that it is there, and that it has a profound influence in life and on our actions.

Two perspectives

One outcome of the internal division is that we see the world as though from two quite different perspectives. We see it as though from 'within', and also as though from 'outside'. Rollo May, a well-known psychologist wrote, "the human dilemma is that which arises out of a man's capacity to experience himself as both subject and object at the same time."[8] He went further and said that a colleague of his had remarked that, as a therapist, he alternated, "as in a tennis game, between seeing the patient as object — when he thinks of patterns, dynamics, reality testing, and other aspects of general principles to which the patient's behavior refers — and as subject, when he empathizes with the patient's suffering and sees the world through the patient's eyes."[9]

We see not only others but also ourselves in a twofold way, which has given rise to the antagonism between science and religion. The scientist claims that seeing the world and human beings from outside, objectively — which really means as objects — is the only legitimate way. He will say that to see these objects as though from within is 'subjective', a word often used in a pejorative way, and which means, to the scientist, a seeing which is biased, unreliable and imaginary. Religion, on the other hand, considers the human being from the point of view of meaning, value and significance, and looks so to say from within.

Both points of view are valid, but, because one is seeing as though from within and the other as though from outside, they are incompatible — which reflects the deeper schism that lies at the heart of our being. Because of the success of the scientific point of view in controlling the physical world, management longs to bring the power of its methodology into the corporate realm. As I shall show, one of the reasons for widespread depression, anxiety and a general sense of meaningless, is our undervaluing the importance of the 'subjective' point of view in the corporate system.

The dilemma

It seems to be an impossible situation. We have the imperative: 'Let there be one', one dynamic center, but we have the fact of two incompatible points of view. The problem can be resolved by alternation: now I see others, myself, and the world as though from inside, that is as though I am the center; now I see them from outside as though I am at the periphery. Or I can ban one of the viewpoints, which means that either one or the other must go, as when we think logically, in an either/or way. Science, in order to be able to develop a consistent set of data, has decreed that only data obtained from outside is legitimate — legitimate, that is, for scientific endeavor. The behaviorist school of psychology, and the neo-Darwinian school in biology, have taken this decree to its ultimate and have mostly banished altogether the subjective, including consciousness itself. Even so most of us, most of the time, try to live with both points view, sometimes with them both active at the same time. The dilemmas and ambiguities that this creates are the reason why life and the work situations are so often so messy and uncontrolled.

The stable center

'I' is a stable center that we create to resolve the conflict inherent in us. Conflict does not arise in consciousness but upstream of it. With the birth of 'I', consciousness as we know it is born. 'I' is a fairly latecomer in the evolution of human consciousness. Before 'I' was born the stable center was provided by the cosmic tree, the totem pole, the sacred mountain or an idol and later by the temple.[10] The cross and the mandala, perfect symbols for depicting the conflict and its resolution at the center, are very ancient symbols. The cross predates Christianity by thousands of years.

The following example will help to underscore the vital importance of having a stable center as point of reference, and show why its loss can generate dire distress.

Suppose you have to make your way through a dense forest. It is quite dark because the sunlight can hardly penetrate the dense bush. You know that if you just keep walking directly north you will get through the forest in a few days. You have enough food for the journey and a compass. All that you need do is to follow the direction the compass is pointing. Suppose further, after a day's travel, you lose confidence in the compass. You wonder if it is really pointing north, the stable point. Every tree is similar to every other tree, and no central or stable point can be found. Not a few people have died from panic because they lost themselves in this way.

In the book *Apollo 13*, which tells the story of that ill-fated space capsule, the authors talk of the eight-ball: "a guidance system containing a stationary component, which contained a stable element that was inertially fixed in space relative to the stars."[11] A gimbal lock, a loss of the stable center in a spacecraft, would be tantamount to having no stable point in a forest of stars and galaxies, and the astronauts would be completely lost in space.

A man who had bouts of mania gives some inkling of a world without a center in the following account:

> Psychosis leaves you with fear; you lose all sense of yourself as a person among other persons. You feel yourself dissipating; your distinctiveness vanishes. No voice in the universe sounds like your voice; yet all voices sound like your voice. You see yourself as a vast multitude; and all these millions in the multitude become you. This voice, this multitude that is me, has a detached quality to it without substance or body. *This multitude drowns me; it swallows me up.* With its persistent hollowness, *the voice blots out any sense of an I* and this hollow sound, like drums beating in a huge cavern, encircles me and paralyzes my thoughts. (Emphasis added)[12]

If we look inside, into immediate experience, we find in ourselves an incipient tension, which fluctuates in intensity, now becoming intense stress perhaps accompanied by anxiety, depression or anger, now becoming just mild dissatisfaction. A continuous stream of thought, an inner mono-duologue accompanies the tension. Although the stream of thought eases the tension to some extent, in its turn it creates a steady sense of wear. We will also notice a tendency to look to the future. We want something to look forward to, or we want to have some project in the future that engages us. This comes from the dynamic nature of our inner life. We look to some future dynamic center with which we can be identified, and which will give us a stable point of reference. When we do not have anything to look forward to we feel flat, disinterested. But, if we begin to lose the dynamic center altogether then we feel anxious or depressed. A woman, writing about her experience of losing the dynamic center, said,

> Just as I reached for each defense, the knowledge that I had not a single weapon dawned in me like a sudden blow to the head, and in the same instant I understood this thing called self [I]; it is man's defense against seeing absolute nothingness, against seeing a world devoid of life, a world devoid of God. *Without a self, a man is defenseless against such a vision,* a vision he cannot possibly live with. (Emphasis added.)[13]

I and mine

'I', the stable center, can be invested. 'I' become identified with whatever it is invested in and it then becomes 'mine', or 'ours'. For example,
people will invest the stable center in a flag. In earlier battles the goal of
an army was to capture the enemy's standard. When the standard was
captured or fell the army would fall into disarray because the center was
lost. In football much of the excitement of the game comes from who is
in control of the ball, the dynamic center of the game. To be in control
and to own are closely associated. Territory is another way of investing
the center. Some of the earliest laws are associated with the possession
of land in order to protect investment. Later, ways that 'I', or the dynamic
center, is invested in the work place will be explored.

The dynamic center is the emissary of Unity, downstream of the split
in our being. Because it represents unity only one dynamic center is
possible. An example of the need for a centre is in the leadership of a
group. The leader of a group to which I belong is the group's center and
he or she is also my center. A clear distinction must be made between a
leader and a manager. Briefly the function of a manager is to organize
the group, while the function of a leader is to be the dynamic center for
that group. Most often, although by no means always, both these two
functions are vested in the same individual. The leader of a group is the
constellating power of the group, the power that holds the members
together in a functional way even though each member may have needs
that conflict with the needs of the other members of the group.

If the power of the center is too weak to hold the group together then
it will break into splinter groups. These groups will each have their own
centers. Each of these centers may well vie to become the leader of the
group as a whole. The members of such a group will be torn between
these conflicting centers. Instead of being able to channel the stress in
creative and productive ways, belonging to the group will create additional stress.

Only one dynamic center, one leader, can exist at any one time. In
the days when astronauts traveled in two-person capsules, one was
always appointed the leader. In the army the one with the highest rank
and the greatest seniority is the leader. This is clearly spelt out and recognized so that, should the leader be killed in action, his successor is
appointed automatically and without delay. Underlying 'only one
dynamic center' is the imperative: let there be One! If two leaders try to
take control, tension and often outright conflict results. Partnerships are
so often difficult because each of the partners may want to be the center.

A group invests the dynamic center in its leader, which is true not only for human beings but for animals as well. Wolves during the breeding season will establish territories, that is to say, they invest the dynamic center in the territory. A male wolf without territory will be impotent. However, after the young have been brought up, the wolves will form packs and one wolf will be adopted as the leader. A leader is someone in whom the followers feel that they can safely invest their dynamic center.

In a truly creative and productive group, the center will move freely from person to person depending upon the needs of the moment. In a poorly structured group much of the energy of the participants will be spent on the struggle to become the center. The less secure someone is, the greater will be the need to hold on to the center. Trying to *be* the center can be a way of doing this; seeking out what appears to be the strongest and most secure center and identifying with that can be another way. A great deal of group dynamics can be understood if one appreciates the power of the center.

For some animals the most central territory is the most valuable and the most powerful member of the group will take control of that territory. In a company the president occupies the central territory, which also explains why the question of whose office is next to the CEO's, that is, who is closest to the dynamic center, the center of power, can be of paramount importance. When the peace talks between the USA and North Vietnam were getting underway, much preliminary time was spent on deciding the shape of table to be used. Eventually a round table was selected. Someone sitting at the head of an oblong table could have been seen as the dynamic center, the leader. King Arthur's roundtable was selected for the same reason. Even a flock of chickens has a strict hierarchy with the leader being the dynamic center of the flock. Thus we get the expression 'the pecking order'.

The unique one

'I', the name given to the dynamic center, is the emissary of dynamic unity. When 'I' am affirmed, the fact that I am unique, the one center, is also affirmed. As the one, 'I' 'stand out', or 'I' am outstanding. *Ego* is Latin for 'I', but ego is also associated with conceit, arrogance, and pride. Each race and nation claims to be unique: the Jews see themselves as the chosen race. But so do the Americans, British, Germans, French, Japanese, Chinese and all the other nations. The Catholics claim to have the only true religion, while the Calvinists go further and claim to be the elect, predestined for heaven. In his book, *On the Closing of the American Mind*, Alan Bloom, says, "[Non-Western cultures] think their way is the best way and all others are inferior . . . One should conclude from the study of non-Western cultures that not only to prefer one's own way but to believe it best, superior to others is primary and even natural."[14] If any one is in doubt about the strength of the claim to be unique, let him tune into a TV broadcast of a soccer game played in a World Cup series, and observe the passionate support each team is given by supporters from the respective country.

I see Canada as unique because I am unique and a Canadian. The difficulty that people had in accepting that the earth was not the center of the universe was a very personal difficulty, not a scientific, or even theological one. The earth is the center of the universe because I am on earth and I am the center of the universe. Darwin's theory suffered the same kind of rejection because it dethroned human beings from being at the pinnacle of creation, as well as from being a divine creation. In dethroning the human being Darwin dethrones me.

All that has been said about the wound, or basic contradiction, and its effects, including the need that it creates for a stable center, will have profound relevance to an understanding of work and organization. However, first we must look at the part that dynamic unity plays in perception, in order to show how creativity and work are grounded in perception and so grounded in human nature. It will also show how creativity and work are grounded in the wound at the heart of our being. In chapter three I will show the connection between perception and creativity, which will enable me to show specifically how creativity is directly related to the basic schism or wound. Then I will put forward how work can be seen as a creative process.

Notes

1 Joel Balkan, *The Corporation: the pathological pursuit of money and power* (Toronto: Penguin, 2004), p. 166.
2 Jaques, *Requisite Management*, p. 10.
3 The first 'noble truth' or basic axiom of Buddhism is "Life is suffering."
4 See Daniel M. Wagener, *The Illusion of Conscious Will* (Cambridge, MA: The MIT Press, 2002).
5 *The Essential Plotinus* Translated with an introduction by Elmer O'Brien (Toronto: Mentor Books, 1964), p. 74.
6 It is said that Adam injured or wounded himself by his sin, and so wounded the human race.
7 *Disgust*, literally means two tastes, *distract*, means drawn apart and *distraught* means to be afflicted with mental conflict.
8 Rollo May, *Psychology and the Human Dilemma* (New Jersey: D. Van Nostrand Co., 1967), p. 8.
9 *Ibid.*, p. 8.

10 Although the importance of the stable center is widely recognized in Japan and China, particularly among those practicing Zen and the Martial arts, few Western thinkers have paid much attention to the important part that it plays in the ecology of being. One psychologist, Carl Jung, does frequently write about it, particularly in reference to the *mandala*. The mandala is a four-pointed symbol with a fifth central point. The word 'mandala' means center and periphery. Jung says that the mandala is an important symbol for self-individuation. The art critic, Rudolph Arnheim, also writes about the dynamic center in his book *The Power of the Center* (Berkeley: California University Press, 1982) in which he shows the importance of the dynamic center in works of art and in architecture.

However, the writer who has most to say about the center is the mythologist, Mircea Eliade. He points out that the center had an enormous importance for the ancients. He says, "Every human being tends, even unconsciously towards the Center, and towards his own center, where he can find integral reality — sacredness. This desire, so deeply rooted in man, to find himself at the very heart of the real — at the Center of the World, the place of communication with Heaven — explains the ubiquitous use of 'Centers of the World.'" Mircea Eliade, *Images and Symbols* (London: Harvill Press, 1961), p. 54.

Shortly after this he says that as human beings we have nostalgia for Paradise. "By this we mean the desire to find oneself always and without effort in the Center of the World, at the heart of reality; and by a short cut and in a natural manner to transcend the human condition, and to recover the divine condition — as the Christian would say, the condition before the fall." The condition before the fall would be Unity before being wounded by ignoring our true source. *Ibid.*, p. 55.

11 Jim Lovell and Jeffrey Kluger, *Apollo 13* (New York: Pocket Books, 1995), p. 127.

12 James M. Glass, *Private Terror/Public Life: psychosis and the politics of community* (Ithaca: Cornell University, 1989), p. 36.

13 Bernadette Roberts, *The Experience of No-self* (Boston: Shambhala, 1984), p. 43.

14 Allan Bloom, *The Closing of the American Mind* (New York: Simon and Schuster, 1987), p. 36.

CHAPTER TWO

On Perception and Thought

In order to be an effective manager, to be able to organize and motivate others and ourselves, we need to know ourselves. In the process we will see that we are naturally creative. In a company, this creativity needs to be channeled through good organization. Moreover, organization is good if it is in harmony with our basic nature. I have shown how we are divided against ourselves, and how our lives are pervaded by a continuous sense of stress and tension. In some, this is felt to be a free-floating anxiety; in others it is felt as a pervasive sense of depression or a simmering sense of anger and rage. Human beings have devised several strategies and ways by which to alleviate, and even to use stress, and one of the most important of these is work.

Good organization enables us to use stress as energy for creativity. This will be the theme of the next few chapters. Work that is well organized also enables us to project goals into the future, and tension is reduced in us when we have something to look forward to. In the previous chapter I emphasized the importance of the center as the most important stress-relieving factor in life. Without a center we can fall into the deepest hell. I have justified saying this in several other books and will not repeat the justification here. The investment of the center is done in a variety of situations. One of the most important of these is work.

What then does saying that tension can be used in a natural, creative and productive way mean? To respond to this question I must show that creativity is natural, that life is creative, not mechanical. We are living beings, not complicated robots, and creativity clearly distinguishes us from robots. Creativity, moreover, is the basis of perception because perception is not simply a question of receiving information through the senses. Perception involves creativity on the one hand, and thought and judgment on the other.

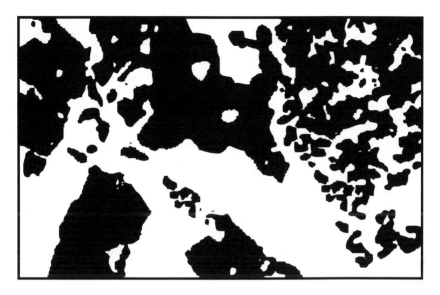

Figure 2.1 Hidden man

The hidden man

When you look at figure 2.1, what do you see? This question will help lay the foundation for much that will follow so I should like you to study the illustration carefully to see how you can answer it. You should not give up too easily. Please do not go on reading until you have studied the illustration and have seen that it is not simply a random collection of shapes but a *very clear picture*. Doing this experiment will show us some distinctive elements of perception and, ultimately, of thought and creation as well. I shall refer back to it constantly throughout the book.

Discussion of the hidden man

When you looked at the illustration probably all that you first saw was a chaotic black and white dissonance, just a random display of irregular black-and-white forms. If you worked long enough you will have then seen a very clear picture of a man, or rather the lower half of the face and the upper torso of a man. He has a beard, and the face is quite pleasant. It could almost be a picture of Christ. If you haven't yet perceived the face I do assure you that the face is clearly there.

The face is not any old face; in other words the exercise is not a variation on the Rorschach test. In the Rorschach test, as you probably know, you are presented with a series of inkblots and encouraged to use your imagination to create pictures or patterns. This illustration is different because a 'best fit' is possible, while the inkblots of the Rorscharsch test do not have a 'best fit'. In the Rorscharsch test you are encouraged to use your imagination; with this exercise *you do not use your imagination.*

You have to work if you want to perceive the face. The work is no different in kind, although considerably different in degree, from the work of organizing a department or developing a system. Some people see the face immediately, but most have to do the work. If you did the work then 'the field of phenomena' — the black-and-white dissonant shapes — became a face. What did you feel when you just saw the chaotic shapes? Did you feel somewhat confused, and see them as meaningless? Did you feel somewhat tense? When you perceived the face, and order had been put into chaos, did you feel a release from tension?

If you had a difficult time when you were trying to see the face you may have noticed that after a while you began to feel tense, even somewhat frustrated and irritated. Some tension must build up in order to do this work properly. Most people get quite tense when faced with chaos or a lack of order. So much so is this the case that people who have been blind from birth and subsequently undergo an operation to have their sight restored, find that the perceptual confusion that greets them is so great, and the work involved in learning how to organize this perceptual confusion so difficult and stressful, that they almost wish they were blind once more. One man, who had had his sight restored, put it this way, "When I could see again, objects literally hurled themselves at me. One of the things a normal person knows from long habit is what *not* to look at. Things that don't matter, or that confuse, are simply shut out of their seeing minds. I had forgotten this, and tried to see everything at once; consequently I saw almost nothing."[1]

Once you saw the face you probably experienced some, perhaps even considerable, relief, a feeling of satisfaction; some have a feeling of surprise, while others even feel amused when the face becomes clear.

The exercise, and the tension that accompanies it, show that we do not like chaos and have a very basic need for order. Moreover the relief that you feel when you see the picture emphasizes how important is order, pattern, structure or organization. The Rorschach test that I referred to earlier is based upon the truth that the human mind always seeks pattern or order. We will even make the ticking of a clock into a pattern: tick-tock-tick-tock, rather than just tick-tick-tick-tick. Mathematicians tell us that it is almost impossible to create randomness deliberately.

The need for order comes from the drive of dynamic unity. Pattern, order, and organization are ways by which randomness is reduced and unity attained. Dynamic unity is therefore the basis of perception, and the fact that the face does not appear gradually in stages confirms this. The face appears complete, whole, or it does not appear at all. Unity cannot appear gradually; one cannot have half of a whole. (Half an apple is still a whole).

If you watch others working, struggling to see the face, you can identify immediately when they have accomplished the work, when they have seen the face a sudden change occurs in them. Many people smile.

The *Gestalt* and analysis

The picture you perceived can be called a *gestalt*. The word '*gestalt*' can mean an integrated whole or 'one'. The *Gestalt* psychologists showed that the human mind does not simply add together random elements or sensations to make a whole, but that a new whole appears complete without any apparent build up. The new whole has properties that do not appear in the parts. An obvious example of a new whole, although there are innumerable others that could be given, is water. The parts of water are hydrogen and oxygen. When these are integrated into a *gestalt* the result, water, has properties such as wetness, viscosity, and a density that the gases did not have. The picture that you saw when integrated into a whole as a face also acquired properties that were not in the parts: the whole has meaning as a face, the face can be likened to the face of Jesus, and the face is incomplete. Similarly we feel life has meaning when it has pattern or coherence.

Analysis, or as it is sometimes called 'reductionism', is a process whereby a whole is reduced to its parts or elements. These elements are units or 'atoms'. The word 'atom' originally meant 'indivisible', or 'one'. The ultimate aim of analysis is to find the units or elements that cannot be divided further. In medicine the unit could be the virus; in physics it is most often these days the particle, although sometimes the vibrating string; in work, as will be shown, the unit is a *task cycle*.

Analysis comes from the activity of dynamic unity, but it goes in the opposite direction to *Gestalt* perception. Whereas the *gestalt* is inclusive, and integrates the elements, analysis is exclusive or reductive and goes in the direction of separating out the elements. The ultimate whole, or *Gestalt*, is the universe; the ultimate atom is a dimensionless point. If you try to imagine the ultimate whole you will need to expand the mind to its limit; to imagine the dimensionless point you will need to concentrate and contract the mind as far as possible. The first is centrifugal; the second is centripetal. Centrifugal/centripetal opposition will be met with quite often throughout our study of work and organization. Sometimes I shall call it *conflict*, at other times I shall refer to it as *incompatibility*,

Although we tend to perceive wholes, the whole that we perceive may not be the optimum. Some people, using their imagination, simply project a face or some other picture on to figure 3.1 in an endeavor to grasp a whole rather than be faced with a confused mess. They do not see the whole as the bearded face of a man. But because they have seen a whole in their way, if one tells them that they have not yet seen the face, they are reluctant to revert back to the original chaos and perceive anew. Indeed some even get angry and insist: 'well it is simply a matter of opinion'. This is called prejudice. We 'make up our minds about something'; in other words, we grasp the situation as a whole, and then tend to listen to, read, and accept what conforms to our *gestalt*; we prejudge from the basis of a given *gestalt*.

Let me repeat, perception, which is based upon information received from outside, is guided by a tendency to perceive units or 'ones'. This tendency to be guided by unity occurs not only when we perceive, but also when we act. If you learn to skate, at first you will make a flurry of unnecessary and random actions. As you become more skilled your skating will become more unified and harmonious.

Perhaps you will recall the quote that I gave earlier from Plotinus: "No army, no choir, no flock exists except that it be one. No house, even, or ship." The army, the flock, the choir are one because we perceive it to be one. You may be surprised by such a statement, so let me ask you to do another experiment. Look at your thumb; now look at your hand; now look at your arm. When you look at your hand, the thumb 'disappears' as a thumb. When you look at your arm, your hand 'disappears' as a hand. If you do not believe me, look at the comma after the word 'me' that is just before the word 'look' in this sentence. Did it not 'appear' for you only after I asked you to look at it, perceive it? Yet the comma modified your reading, even before it 'appeared'. Thus we can see that the unity — the thumb, the hand, and the arm — is a creation; it is not a property of what we perceive.

The hand is both a whole, and it is a part of the arm. Arthur Koestler[2] coined the useful word *holon* that means both *gestalt* and element, whole and part. A company is a holon: it is a whole but also part of society. Departments within a company, and jobs within a department are also holons. One of the great obstructions to creative thought is the insistence on either/or. Here the insistence is that something is either an element or a whole. Much of the mechanistic theory of today arises from just this insistence. Such thinking claims that the only legitimate way to think is to break wholes down into their elements and that the elements are the basic reality. As we shall see, 'either/or' thinking permeates thinking about a company and its organization, as well as about ourselves.

To sum up

The example of seeing the hidden man is an example of perception. Perception is often thought to be simply seeing with the senses. The example shows that perception includes the activity of the senses (seeing, hearing, tasting, smelling are involved in perceiving), but it also includes an activity of the 'mind'. Each of us experiences the world not as it is, but as we construct it, and each constructs it differently. This lays the way open for misunderstanding, disagreement and conflict.

Working on figure 3.1 also shows us something else: the creative process is not a conscious one. Nor is the drive to unity a conscious drive, as I pointed out in the previous chapter. On the contrary, consciousness is a result of the drive to unity. Consciousness is awareness, memory, present experience, and language, organized around a unique, dynamic center by dynamic unity.

In chapter five I will discuss a spectrum of mental processes that affect perception; we shall see that many levels of perception are possible and that each has a characteristic process of the mind associated with it. Before going on to that, first let me show how perception and creativity are intimately connected. I will start by giving an example of creativity and then clarify what I mean by the word 'creativity'.

Notes

1 K. F. Muenzinger, *The Psychology of Behavior* (New York: Harper, 1942).
2 Arthur Koestler, *The Ghost in the Machine* (London: Pan Books, 1967), p. 65.

CHAPTER THREE

The Meaning of Creativity

Perception is the foundation of work and of our organization of work. Indeed, perception is its own kind of work, its own kind of organization. Work is a natural way by which we use and reduce the stress in life. Basically stress is brought about by the fundamental schism, the contradiction that lies at the heart of our being. This schism is the original dissonance. Perception helps heal the wound by offering coherent, unified experience. Our experience of the world is through wholes, but these wholes too can be in conflict with each other. The whole that I perceive as a manager, the whole that I perceive as a father and the whole that I perceive as a husband may well be in conflict. Some people feel irritated or acutely uncomfortable when going from the work situation to the home situation. Even so, perception is basic to all these situations. Let us now move on and ask what the word 'creativity' means. Such an enquiry will help to show that human beings are naturally creative.

Creativity is not confined to genius

Many people believe that the word 'creativity' refers to some kind of mystical activity, some special ability that only a few fortunate people have, something that they are born with. These people tend to believe that you either have it or you don't; you are either a creative person or you are not. Creativity, we are often told, is closely associated with imagination or vision and, not knowing quite what these mean, we just agree that only artists are gifted with them. Creativity is also said to be close to madness, and so we wonder whether after all being creative is a good idea.

I want to show that the mind is essentially creative, and that creativity is not a rarity but ongoing at all levels of life and at all times in a life. Although sometimes imagination and vision may play a part in creativity, they are not essential. What I will also show is that some of the misconceptions about the creative process come from the way society teaches us to think logically and analytically: break a problem down into its component parts, and then find the relation between these parts using the rules of logic.

Society generally takes for granted that the logical/analytical way of thinking is the only real way to think. The reason that it seems to be so unassailable is because, many believe, it mirrors the way the world is. For example, analytically cells can be reduced to molecules, and so it is believed that cells are 'really' molecules. Scientists feel that if they can understand the behavior of molecules, then they will have the key to understanding all life. One biologist for example said, "A great deal of the universe does not need any explanation. Elephants for instance. Once molecules have learnt to compete with other molecules in their own image, elephants, and things resembling elephants, will in due course be found roaming through the countryside."[1] In the days of Frederick Taylor and the Gilbreths, industry was reorganized through the reductionist process of analyzing work into the smallest possible compo-nent[2] and then organizing those components along a conveyor belt. They ushered in mass production.

Creative thought, which has a great deal in common with *gestalt* thinking or holism, has become marginalized, is considered to be a rarity and often looked upon with suspicion. I will come back later to the connection between the way society teaches us to think and creativity and discuss it in more detail, but first, let me say what I mean by the word 'creativity'.

Definition of creativity

A well-known writer and essayist who wrote in the forties and fifties, Arthur Koestler, said that creativity occurs when a *single* situation or idea is perceived in "two self consistent but habitually *incompatible* frames of reference."[3]

James Beatty, an eighteenth-century English poet, gave a similar description of humor. He said that it arose "from the view of two or more inconsistent, unsuitable, or incongruous parts or circumstances, consid-ered as united in one complex object or assemblage."[4] The connection between humor and creativity is underlined by a Hermetic text, which tells us that the world was created by laughter.[5]

Many other definitions and ways of talking about creativity are possible but I will use Koestler's definition because it is most apt for what I have to say about work and a company.

Creativity, choice and calculation

Let us clearly distinguish between *creativity*, *choice* and *calculation* by looking at an example that involves all three.

During renovations that I was doing on a building I found that the dimensions of the existing staircase did not conform to the building code and had to be rebuilt. Yet, if I built it according to the code, the staircase would have to go through the facing wall, which was quite impractical. If I did not build it according to the code, the building inspector would not approve the construction. These two alternatives were completely incompatible . . . so what could I do?

In constructing the staircase the first problem was to *calculate* how high the stairs had to go, how many stairs would be needed to go that high, and how much ground space would be necessary to accommodate that number of stairs. After having done so I could clearly see the problem mentioned above and so had to find a *creative* resolution for it. Later, after having found this resolution, I would have to *choose* the materials of which the staircase would be made. For example, a hard wood, like oak, or a soft wood, like pine could equally well be used.

Three different kinds of problems therefore presented themselves: a problem that called for calculation, another that called for choice, and a third that called for creativity.

Calculation

I had had no difficulty discovering the size of the staircase and space for the staircase. I simply calculated them. The height of each stair had to be eight inches, and the tread or depth of the stair had to be ten. The code specifies these dimensions. To obtain the number of stairs that had to be installed, I simply measured how high the stairs had to go to reach the next floor and divided that height by eight inches. To calculate how deep the staircase had to be I multiplied the number of stairs we needed, (given by the first calculation) by ten inches. This involved a straightforward calculation taught early in grade school.

Calculation has therefore two distinct characteristics that distinguish it from creativity: the solution that one arrives at is either right or wrong; a set of procedures, such as addition, multiplication, subtraction or division, gives one the solution.

Choice

Let us now consider the differences between choice and calculation. Choice has no set procedure like calculation by which to arrive at an answer. Furthermore, when choosing material for the stairs one seeks an *appropriate* and not a *right* choice. One uses such criteria as cost, convenience, aesthetics, and durability, among others. The difference between a solution based on calculation and one based on choice is quite obvious; the difference between choice and creativity is not so clear.

Creativity

I had two constraints: the dimensions of the staircase, which were fixed by the building code, and the dimensions of the space within which to build the staircase. These were, to use Koestler's expression, *incompatible frames of reference*. But a staircase had to be built: this was Koestler's *single idea*. Therefore the problem called for a creative solution. A spiral staircase would have solved the problem, although it would have had to be made of metal and would not have been very aesthetic. I thought of putting the staircase in another part of the building altogether, but logistically such a solution would have created a number of difficulties. I could have done away with the staircase and put in a small elevator. This would have been too costly. All these are creative suggestions and each could, at a stretch, have been used. So a creative solution, just like an answer based upon choice, cannot be judged according to whether it is right or wrong, but only according to how appropriate it is. And, just like choice, no set procedures are available for arriving at the solution. So where do choice and creativity differ?

The dilemma

Perhaps the difference becomes obvious if one says that creativity is required when a *dilemma* and not a *problem* confronts us. Choice, on the other hand, is concerned with a problem. When confronted by a dilemma you are 'damned if you do, and damned if you do not'. If I built according to the code, I would be damned, because the staircase would have to go through the facing wall; if I did not build according to the code I would be damned, because the building inspector would not agree with what I had done. I *have* to choose between the two alternatives; but I *cannot* choose one alternative over the other.

A choice does not carry with it such a dilemma. Suppose, for the sake of simplicity, that oak and pine are the only kinds of wood available. Let us say that these two are all that the store has in stock. Again, two alternatives are available — oak instead of pine, or pine instead of oak. But this time I can choose between the two; nothing stops me in the way that one or the other horn of a dilemma stops me. With a dilemma, both alternatives must be chosen, but both cannot be chosen. Yet, I reject one or the other at my peril. But with a choice I can reject one alternative, say the oak, in favor of the other alternative of pine.

When discussing work I shall show that all the jobs in a company, from the most menial to the most senior, have what could be called a *managerial aspect* and a *technical aspect*. The managerial aspect is concerned with dilemmas and has creativity as an important ingredient. The technical aspect includes those tasks that are performed in a prescribed or habitual way, and these are tasks for which a right or wrong answer can be found. Choice falls midway between managerial activity and technical activity. As one ascends the management hierarchy so the proportion of managerial work relative to technical work increases.

Creativity and humor

As creativity and humor share the same structure, humor can help deepen our understanding of the meaning of creativity. Here, as examples to show what I mean, are some actual announcements that appeared on the bulletin boards of various churches.

> "Thursday night — Potluck supper. Prayer and medication will follow."

> "This being Easter Sunday, we will ask Mrs. Lewis to come forward and lay an egg on the altar."

> "For those of you who have children and don't know it, we have a nursery downstairs."

Each of these statements can be read in two equally valid, but quite incompatible ways. You have to choose one way to read it over the other, but, initially at least, you cannot choose one over the other because both appear at the same time. If you do not see the two alternatives simultaneously then you do not see the joke.

More on dilemmas

A dilemma that most adolescents encounter is the freedom/security dilemma. On the one hand, the child wants to be free of restraint to do as he pleases; on the other hand, he wants the security of the home. Another dilemma that we all face is both wanting to be unique, separate, distinct, yet also wanting to be part of a group, to fit in and go along with the crowd. Another set of dilemmas is the following: if you want A you have to give up B; yet B is as attractive as A. The young woman knows that if she gives her affection to one man, she will have to deny it to all the others. Yet among all the others there may be just the right man. If I take a job, then all the other jobs are denied me. A saying that sums it up well: "He wants to have his cake and eat it." Most of us have faced variations of these dilemmas.

When organizing a company one sometimes has to decide whether to centralize or decentralize. Centralizing enables one to maintain control, to have common standards, and to speed up communication about decisions. Decentralizing gives greater freedom and autonomy to the departments, encourages local initiative, and gives greater flexibility. Another similar dilemma is whether to organize by function or by product. I shall give a number of other dilemmas later.

Our lives tend to be frustrating because often, although faced with dilemmas, we believe that we are faced with choices: perhaps one horn of the dilemma is not so obvious as the other; or perhaps to see one or other horn as legitimate is too painful. Only later, sometimes even after a decision has been made, do we realize that we were in fact faced with a dilemma and not a choice. One of the reasons that many do not trust politicians is that that they appear to be faced with choices when in fact they are often caught up in dilemmas.

The struggle against terrorism, which the West is currently waging, is fraught with dilemmas. As George Friedman pointed out in his book *America's Secret War*, the attacks on the US embassies in Kenya and Tanzania were designed to test the reaction of the US. He said, "The Clinton administration was caught on the horns of a dilemma. If it did not respond, Al Q'aida's credibility would rise in the Islamic world. If it did respond, it would set in motion the process that Al Q'aida hoped for."[6]

The attack on the World Trade Center left George W. Bush no room to maneuver and he was faced with a dilemma. To quote Friedman again, "At the heart of the homeland defense there is this question: Is this a war or a criminal investigation?"[7] As he goes on to say, the answer is crucial. If it is war then the Geneva Convention of 1949 will apply. If it is a criminal investigation then the Justice system will be brought into play, neither of which are desirable from Bush's point of view, and yet one or other must apply. "The problem was that this war was being waged inside the United States. The practice of capturing people in the

United States — including American citizens — and treating them as military captives not covered by the Geneva Convention raised hackles everywhere."[8]

The war on Iraq initially put the Bush administration in yet another quandary: was it a covert war, run by intelligence organizations or was it a military operation? If the former then it had to have complex and unstated goals; if the latter it had to have very clear goals. "The administration's public presentation of this war was trapped by this dilemma."[9]

Creativity and conflict

It is quite obvious that dilemmas are situations in which a single idea is called upon to resolve two incompatible frames of reference. The conditions of creativity, therefore, have two parts: a single, unifying idea, and at least two conflicting frames of reference, although more than two may be involved. In future, when appropriate, I will call these contradictory frames of reference *dissonance*. The single idea is a manifestation of the drive to unity with which we are now familiar.

The word dissonance carries overtones of conflict. Conflict and creativity have the same fundamental structure, and conflict is necessary for creativity to be possible. When Koestler speaks of creativity he says the situation, "vibrates simultaneously on two different wavelengths," and he coins a word *bisociation* to refer to this way of perceiving. The two mutually incompatible frames of reference generate a tension, which explodes at the moment of creation. To describe creative tension Koestler uses words such as 'clash', 'explosion', 'collision', 'confrontation'; words that can just as well, indeed often do, describe conflict.

Koestler's definition of creativity is very similar to Kenneth Boulding's definition of conflict: the "incompatibility of the position of the two parties"; and unity: "the single position to which each is aspiring."[10] Both creativity and conflict are made up of two (or more) incompatible frames of reference, and of unity. As conflicts are very often resolved by some kind of violence we can infer that violence sometimes comes from a failure to find a creative resolution. This means that structures of creativity, humor, dilemma, conflict and some violence are isomorphic.

Conflict lies at the heart of creativity, while unity lies in the heart of conflict. Conflict and creativity both have the peculiar property of arising out of unity that is at the same time a duality: out of a duality whose two aspects are seen simultaneously as Unity. Such is true also of a dilemma, of humor and of violence. It is, as I shall show, also true of work, and is one reason why mental work is hard.

Why work is hard

A very simple form of the creative process was your struggle to see the hidden man. Although given as an exercise in perception, it was also an exercise in creativity as well as in work because you probably had to work for a while to see the face. The work arose because on the one hand all that you could see was a mess of black and white; on the other you had my assurance that those black and white shapes were really a clear picture of half of a face. You were presented with two incompatible frames of reference. As you worked and struggled you no doubt would have wanted just to give up, but curiosity prompted you to go on to see the face. If I had simply told you that the illustration was an interesting array of black and white shapes, no struggle or tension would have arisen. The two incompatible frames of reference are the conditions that made the work possible. The categorical imperative, Let there be One! provides the drive to stay with the problem of seeing the face. The categorical imperative gives us the drive to do work, and this imperative operating in two incompatible frames of reference makes for the struggle and also makes work hard.

Suppose that the black and white shapes were a set of mathematical equations that had no obvious connection, but which nevertheless a mathematician guessed somehow were indeed connected. The incompatible frames of reference are, on the one hand the apparent randomness, on the other the possibility of order. A mathematician could spend weeks, months, even years struggling to find the relation between the equations. Fermat's last theorem, a very famous mathematical problem that was only recently resolved, provides an example. Mathematicians worked and struggled for 450 years before a proof could be demonstrated.

Having established the structure of creativity, I can take the next step and show how work too has the same one-but-two structure. First, let me give a preliminary definition that will be used throughout the book: *work is the exercise of discretion within limits in order to produce a result.* Much of chapter six will be devoted to expanding on this definition, and then to showing how this definition enriches our understanding of a company organization. For reasons that I shall give, the limits are incompatible. The exercise of discretion requires commitment and dedication to the task at hand. Commitment is an expression of dynamic unity. Thus work is commitment and dedication within conflicting limits to producing a result.

To sum up

In this chapter we have seen that creativity, work, conflict and even humor have the same basic one/two structure. Seeing this will provide some very valuable insights into the way work can be organized. Creativity and work are but an extension of perception and are intrinsic to life. Both are ways by which one can use tension in a productive way, and so work is natural to us. We can say then that a company is not, as is almost universally claimed, just in business to make a profit for the shareholder. The roots of the company are to be found in the creativity of people and their need to work to express this creativity.

Notes

1 Richard Dawkins, *The Blind Watchmaker* (Harmondsworth: Penguin, 1988), p. 14.
2 The Gilbreths called these units *therbligs*. This is their name in reverse.
3 Arthur Koestler, *The Act of Creation* (London: Pan Books, 1964), p. 35.
4 Barry Sanders, *A is for Ox* (New York: Vintage Books), p. 89.
5 Brian P. Copenhaver *Hermetica* (Cambridge: Cambridge University Press, 1992), p. 97.
6 George Friedman, *America's Secret War: Inside the hidden world struggle between America and its enemies* (New York: Broadway Books, 2004), p. 38.
7 *Ibid.*, p. 121.
8 *Ibid.*, p. 123.
9 *Ibid.*, p. 135.
10 Kenneth Boulding, *Conflict and Defense* (New York: Harper and Row, 1962), p. 5.

CHAPTER 4

Ambiguity, Creativity and Work

On logic

We live life as though a world is 'out there', and I am 'in here'. As a rule the dualist view is taken for granted without a great deal of thought being given to it. We generally believe that it represents the world as it really is and overlook the truth that the dualism comes from the way that we perceive and experience the world. That the world is a collection of things, and that we are one of the things in the world, we also take for granted. This is so because we adopt the objective way of viewing the world, the way that sees a world out there.[1] We believe further that we have an inner world inhabited by thoughts, wishes and dreams. Our belief in these two worlds has it origin in the two ways of viewing the world discussed in chapter one. The dualistic attitude furthermore has become enshrined in a way of thinking, or logic, that is sometimes called *Aristotelian* logic and sometimes called *classical* logic.

Classical logic has three basic principles: x is x, x is A or not A, x cannot be both A and not A. These seem so self-evident that one might wonder how they could ever be challenged.[2] An apple is an apple; a company is a company; I am I. An animal is either a dog or not a dog; it cannot be both a dog and not a dog. How could anyone question these principles or want to find another logic? To challenge such a way of thinking would be to challenge the very foundation of our knowledge, and of our way of seeing the world. We are convinced that the world contains houses and cars, trees and mountains, cats and dogs, apples and pears and all the rest.

Yet, logical thinking stifles creativity because it says x is either A or not A, it cannot be both; that is to say, incompatible frames of reference are unacceptable. The question then arises whether a logic of creativity is possible? If so, it would free us from the shackles of classical logic and show the way for us to be seen as we truly are: as dynamic, creative beings. Let us then take a further look at classical logic and see its limitations, and then we can go on to discuss an alternative way of using the mind.

on/off thinking

Let us call logical thinking, on/off thinking, as to do so will unburden it of some of its mystique. 'Aristotelian logic', 'classical logic', these words belong in the ivory tower, but on/off brings it down to something as simple as a switch. A light is on or off. We must not underestimate the power of on/off thinking. For some time the fastest growing industry has been the electronics industry. This fast growth is quite obvious in the home entertainment field, in computers and in communications. A very simple way of thinking, a thinking that is called *binary* logic (and what I am now simply calling on/off thinking) has, in part, made development possible in computer and allied technology.

Before the computer was developed we used machines called *Hollerith* machines. An operator would pass cards, which had been previously punched with appropriate holes, through these machines and, as the card passed through, a switch would be held in an 'off' position by the card until the hole appeared. When the hole appeared the switch would make contact through the hole and, for that moment, the switch would be 'on'. A counter tallied the number of times the switch was 'on' and 'off'. Because the holes corresponded to data, it was an effective, but limited way of processing information.

The same 'on/off' logic is the logic of the computer. The switches are turned off and on electronically, so to say, and so the calculations can be done much faster, but the principle remains the same.

This kind of thinking is not normally called 'on/off thinking' but logical thinking, or, sometimes, 'either/or' thinking. According to it everything is either one thing or another, either black or white, either right or wrong, male or female, young or old, possible or not possible. We feel comfortable with classical logic. We have the feeling of certainty because of it; moreover, engineers and scientists depend upon it. A measurement is either right or wrong and thousands of lives could well depend upon whether it is right and not wrong. Because of technology on/off thinking has come to have an enormous influence upon our lives, many people claim it to be the only legitimate way to think and that other ways are wrong, or at least inferior. Because so many believe that it is the only right way, and because machines can simulate it and do it so much faster and more accurately than human beings can, the myth has now taken hold that machines will soon outstrip human beings and will ultimately be in control.

The problems with logical thought

As we think and speak about the world so we see the world, and as we see the world so we think and speak about it. When I encountered the problem of the staircase I encountered something fixed, given to me to work with: stairs of a given dimension, and a given dimension of space into which the staircase must fit. I could definitely not do anything about the dimensions of the stairs, and I felt just the same about the space: it had a fixed volume. Finally, after a great deal of thought it occurred to me that perhaps I might be able to do something about the space. In a moment of inspiration I thought, "Why not bring the floor down to the height that the stairs could reach without going through the facing wall?" Such an idea seemed to be an absurd solution because I could not help thinking about the situation in terms of what was given. Then the next piece of the puzzle fell into place: build a landing, put in a couple of stairs down to the landing, and then the floor is, in a way, lowered.

While not a very profound example of creativity, nevertheless it makes the point that one way to be creative is to break up that first principle of classical logic x = x: *everything is what it is*, a statement that has implicit in it 'everything *must* be as it is'. To say an apple is an apple is to forget that that is the way we think about the apple. We then come to believe that that is how the apple is and must be; and, furthermore that that too is how the world is and must be. People have come up with many ways to stimulate creativity such as 'thinking outside the box', 'brainstorming', and 'lateral' thinking, among others. Most of these ways encourage us to challenge the way we habitually think, challenge us to break the rules, so to say. But thinking outside the box still keeps classical logic enshrined. The box obviously is logic; the logic is the rules. With a logic of creativity we would not have to think outside the box any more: we would be rid of the box!

Not only does the way we think inhibit creativity, but, should a disagreement arise then we believe that either one or the other of the parties must be wrong, and so confrontational conflict becomes the real way to resolve conflict. While it is true that we do sometimes compromise, or find creative ways to resolve disagreements, we do so in spite of the firm belief that either you or I have to be wrong, that both cannot be right. Our compromises and creative solutions often seem to be in way a failure to get at, and resolve, the real problem.

Finally our way of thinking prevents us from differentiating between problems and dilemmas. It pushes us into believing that a solution is always possible, even though we may be faced with dilemmas, which cannot be solved, instead of problems that can be.

Definition of ambiguity

Ambiguous thinking is generally considered to be shoddy thinking, and if one encounters it in a scientific or philosophic argument we usually conclude the thinker has failed to follow through sufficiently with his thinking. For example, the following comes from a popular book on thinking and logic: "to tolerate contradiction [or ambiguity] is to be indifferent to truth. For the person who, whether directly or by implication, knowingly both asserts and denies one and the same proposition, shows by that behavior that he does not care whether he asserts what is false and not true, or whether he denies what is true and not false . . . for whenever and wherever I tolerate self-contradiction, then and there I make it evident, either that I do not care at all about truth, or that at any rate I do care about something else more."[3]

Because of the conviction that only logical thinking is clear thinking we have come to believe also that the word 'ambiguity' must mean vague and hazy; but I do not use the word in such a way. I use it to assert and deny one and the same proposition. The word has its origins in *ambi*, meaning two faces. Here is a well-known *Gestalt* illustration, which I will use to illustrate ambiguity:

If we study the illustration for a moment two faces appear: one the face of a young woman, the other the face of an old woman. Seeing

Figure 4.1 Old and young woman

the old woman, we do not see the young woman; seeing the young woman, we do not see the old woman. Only one face is apparent at a time. Each of these two — the young and the old woman — is a valid interpretation of the black and white field; each is the One. But, because of the other, each of these two faces is not the One. Thus the two faces are mutually exclusive, or to use the expression of Koestler and Boulding, they are 'incompatible'.

Suppose now one were to ask, "Which is 'the right' face?" We have just been told that to assert and deny the same proposition is shoddy thinking, so logically they both cannot be right. Suppose that one person said the old woman was the right one and another said it was the young woman. This would be just a mild disagreement without much drama. Yet consider the following: it is an actual case study.

A company decided that the building in which its head office was housed was far too small, and a new building had to be constructed. The old building was in a small provincial town far from Toronto, the center of action. Executives frequently had to fly or drive to Toronto, stay one or more nights in a hotel, and then journey back home when their business was done. Several problems arose because of this. The executives were frequently away from home and their office. The traveling costs were quite high and considerable time was wasted in traveling to and fro. The answer to these problems would be to build or lease a new Head Office in Toronto.

The company had its roots deep in the provincial town. It had been there for about fifty years and if the head office were to move the community would suffer quite severe economic distress. The employees were also very reluctant to move and resistance came from people throughout the hierarchy. The cost of housing was very high in Toronto relative to the provincial town. Whereas in the town the employees would spend five to ten minutes traveling to work, in Toronto they could well spend up to an hour. The management was faced with a dilemma. The 'young woman' says move; the 'old woman' says stay. The discussions were no longer mild, and plenty of drama erupted; on occasions the discussions became serious conflicts.

Logic insists that one or other of these two alternatives had to be the right one and much of the discussions circled around the question: which was the right answer. But, the two alternatives were incompatible and demanded a creative answer, not a logical one. Had this been recognized from the start the discussions would have been quite different, no less intense perhaps, but the intensity would have been constructive and not destructive, as it sometimes turned out to be.

The wave/particle ambiguity

Modern physics has its own young/old woman ambiguity, the wave/particle ambiguity. The physicist, Werner Heisenberg, put the problem thus: "[Matter wave and particle] pictures are of course mutually exclusive, because a certain thing cannot at the same time be a particle (i.e. substance confined to a very small volume) and a wave (i.e. a field spread out over a large space.)"[4] In other words, scientists are telling us that we can no longer take for granted, as have generations of people before us, that the structure of logic and the structure of the world are the same.

Heisenberg's mentor, Neils Bohr, developed a *principle of complementarity* to cope with the anomaly; a principle that he felt would leave classical logic intact. However, it did not help matters very much as it seemed to introduce an arbitrary way of thinking. He seemed to be suggesting that as far as possible we should use classical logic. But, when this creates a problem, for example with the wave/particle duality, then we should use complementary thinking. So two authors, one a historian of science, named Robert Nadeau, and the other a physicist named Menas Kafatos, in order to overcome the difficulty, developed criteria that must be met if Bohr's principle of complementarity is to be both necessary and useful. These criteria are, "(1) the theory consists of two individual and whole constructs (2) the constructs preclude one another in a description of the unique physical phenomenon to which they both apply (3) the complete situation cannot be reached through an addition of the two constructs."[5]

The old woman/young woman illustration meets these criteria perfectly: the two "individual and whole constructs" are the young and the old woman. They "preclude" one another because if you see the young woman you do not see the old woman. Finally adding the two pictures together does not give "the complete situation"; the complete situation is the black and white shapes.

Nadeau and Kafatos criteria validate the different kind of thinking that I am proposing and which I call the *logic of ambiguity*, a way of thinking that management should know about.

I said earlier that a basic principle in logical thinking is that x is either A or not A, and quoted, "wherever I tolerate self-contradiction, then and there I make it evident, either that I do not care at all about truth." Let us say that x is the young /old woman illustration. When I perceive x, I perceive a picture of a young woman and yet the picture is not of a young woman (because it is a picture of an old woman). Yet I am told that I cannot say this, I cannot assert and deny the same proposition, because if I do then I do not care at all about truth. What I *perceive* is not the problem; the problem lies in the limitations that logic imposes on what I can say about what I perceive.

Is a company in business to make a profit for the stockholders or is it in business, as Peter Drucker once said, to provide a service to the community? Our rules of thinking say it has to be one or the other, and most people obey those rules: therefore a company must be in business to make a profit for its stock holders. American corporate law says so and so do most other people who write about corporations. They are quite sure that it cannot equally serve the community and make a profit — one or other of these must be primary: the stockholder; while the other is secondary: a stakeholder: one is the real reason, the real cause; the other is simply the consequence.

An ambiguity within the ambiguity

When we were working on the hidden man we saw first the confused black and white field and out of that the face emerged. Figure 4.1, the young/old woman, also starts as a black and white field, although this field is not quite so obvious, because the young woman and old woman are such ready ways of structuring it.

When looking at figure 4.1 the question arose, "Is the illustration a picture of a young or old woman?" But, with equal justice, is the question, "Is figure 4.1 a black and white field or is it the picture of a young/old woman?" (I will use [/] to indicate an ambiguity.) These two alternatives give a further ambiguity. To state the ambiguity completely: black and white field/(old woman/young woman). Furthermore, the black and white field is single — *one* black and white field. I can therefore use it to stand for dynamic unity, and will use the two faces to stand for any two incompatible frames of reference.

Generalizing on what has been said so far, let me now formulate the logic of ambiguity as follows: "an ambiguity, one face of which (unity) says there is no ambiguity; the other face (duality) says there is ambiguity. Simply stated the logic of ambiguity is One/(yes/no), or one/two.

The logic of ambiguity has the same one-that-is-two structure as creativity and so the logic of ambiguity can be added to the list of isomorphisms. Creativity, perception, humor, work, conflict and now the logic of ambiguity are isomorphic. The logic of ambiguity is therefore the logic of creativity, humor, perception, work and conflict. To think creatively we need a logic other than classical logic, a logic of ambiguity; likewise, to do work — exercise discretion within limits to produce a result — the logic of ambiguity is needed.

Unfortunately the illustration of the young/old woman is static and not dynamic and so it fails to show a very important point. Unity itself is not one but two, an ambiguity dwells within the ambiguity. On the one hand, the One embraces the universe as an all-inclusive, centrifugal, One; on the other hand, the One is concentrated in a dimensionless point as the all exclusive, centripetal, One. I should therefore refine the definition of the logic of ambiguity by saying that *there is an ambiguity one face of which says there is an ambiguity, the other says there is not, but this face is itself ambiguous.*[6]

The logic of ambiguity, one could therefore say, is the 'anatomy' of dynamic unity itself. Unity is not simply a static container, or an abstract concept, but is intensely vibrant, dynamic and creative. This is so because unity is inherently ambiguous. I must add a cautionary note. Although I speak of unity being this or that, I do not infer that unity 'is' something, some ghost-like spirit. Perhaps it would be better to say again that unity is the intensely vibrant, dynamic and creative, categorical imperative — *Let there be One!* — that we call life.

The logic of ambiguity is the logic of life, and of our every day mind. If you remember, in chapter one I said, "The drama of life arises because we are not only one, we are also two: in the very core of our being we are divided against ourselves." Basically life expresses the drive to unity, a dynamic unity that can be called will, commitment or intention and which we have been illustrating by using the black and white shapes. The yes/no, illustrated by the young/old woman, unmediated is the source of stress and anguish. This stress, in the absence of a creative solution, can spiral in and become violent inner conflict, and so create a feeling of intolerable anxiety and panic, even horror.

Work, creativity and the logic of ambiguity as systems

One final idea remains to be explored before finishing chapter four: the idea of a system. The notion of systems thinking is now so familiar that one might find it hard to believe that it is, relatively speaking, a newcomer in the field of thought. Cybernetics, information theory, game theory, decision theory, systems engineering, and operations research, among many other disciplines based upon systems theory are now commonplace.

The progress in computer technology has encouraged us to think in terms of systems rather than in terms of isolated units. This has often forced us to re-examine what we are doing, and to find more rational ways of doing it. In the process the time-honored way of analyzing a system into its parts, and then understanding each part with the hope that doing so will provide an understanding of the whole, no longer applies. Surprisingly enough, though, analytical thinking as the only way of thinking still has some strong adherents in biology who protest that 'holism' is a mystical way of understanding the world, and has no place in science.

In the fifties and sixties a German biologist, Ludwig von Bertalanffy did considerable research on systems theory and finally published his findings in 1968 in a book called *General Systems Theory*.[7] At about the same time in England, J. G. Bennett, a mathematician and philosopher, was developing *Systematics*, an allied although independent study in systems thinking. I will be using Bennett's definition of a system: *a set of independent but mutually related elements*.[8] The definition that I have given of work, creativity, perception, humor, conflict, the logic of ambiguity and the mind show that each is a system. Later Bennett's definition of a system will help us to understand the organization of a company. Organizing in fact demands that we recognize the company as a system, a fact that, because of the prevalence of analytical reductive thinking, can be overlooked and undue emphasis be given to just one of its elements: the bottom line.

Bertalanffy was concerned about the misuse of analytical thinking and classical logic, and was keenly aware of its dangers when carried too far. He felt the necessity of making a change in the way we think. Complexities, wholes and systems, are inherent in all fields of knowledge, a fact that is particularly important and must be remembered in a study of corporations. He said that the "system problem is essentially the problem of the limitation of analytical procedures in science."[9] He felt that analysis and reduction are only useful when the relations between the elements are either non-existent or so weak that they had no real influence.

Bennett's definition shows that the *relations* in a system are just as important as the *elements* of the system. Those who claim that the analytical, reductionist method is the only legitimate scientific method often overlook this truth. The statement that the whole is greater than the sum of its parts, which many reductionists dismiss, is true because the relations are as essential to a system as are the elements. The relations make the system greater than the sum of its elements. Furthermore, as Bertalanffy pointed out, while we can conceive of a sum as being composed gradually, "a system as a total of parts with its interrelations has to be conceived of as being composed instantly."[10] We have already been acquainted with suddenness when we worked on the Hidden Man.

Finally he said, and this is very important in our study, that a consequence of the existence of general system properties is the appearance of structural similarities or *isomorphisms* in different fields.[11] I have already made reference to this consequence when I pointed out that isolating isomorphisms enables us to use the understanding that we have of one system.

Summary

In this chapter I have introduced the *logic of ambiguity*. While analytical thinking is essential for resolving problems, nevertheless to adhere to it as the only way to think inhibits, even stifles, creative thinking. Such an inhibition also makes it very difficult to think about work and organization in a realistic way. Another logic, the logic of ambiguity, is essential if we are to overcome this inhibition and so think clearly about work and its organization.

In the next chapter I will show how creative thinking and logical thinking fit into the overall complexity that we call the mind.

Notes

1   The Hopi Indian language does not have nouns. It only has verbs. This means that the Hopi Indian would see the world quite differently to the way we do. Furthermore, ancient Hebrew did not have a word for a thing, they too would have seen the world quite differently to the way that we see it.

2   The principle of identity was challenged by Alfred Korzybski in his book *Science and Sanity: An introduction to non-Aristotelian systems and General Semantics* (Lancaster: The International non-Aristotelian Library Publishing Company, 1941).

3   Andrew Flew, *Thinking about Thinking* (Glasgow: Fontana, 1975), p. 15.

4   Werner Heisenberg, *Physics and Philosophy: The Revolution in Modern Science* (New York: Harper Torchbooks, 1958), p. 49.

5   Robert Nadeau and Menas Kafatos, *The Non-local Universe: The new physics and matters of the mind* (New York: Oxford University Press, 1999), p. 95.

6   Another, more elegant, definition would read: the logic of ambiguity has one face that is ambiguous in principle (old/young woman) but unambiguous in expression (either young or old woman); it has another face that is unambiguous in principle (unity) but ambiguous in expression (inclusive and exclusive unity).

7   Ludwig von Bertalanffy, *General System Theory* (New York: George Braziller, 1968).

8   J. G. Bennett, *The Dramatic Universe, Vol. III* (London: Hodder & Stoughton, 1966). Bennett's study provides some of the theoretical underpinning of the ideas explored in this book. The definition of a system is taken from his work.

9 Von Bertalanffy, *General Systems Theory: Foundations, Development, Applications*, p. 18.
10 *Ibid.*, p. 55.
11 *Ibid.*, p. 80.

CHAPTER FIVE

The Spectrum of Creativity, Perception and Thought

Summary so far

The 'drive' to unity is paramount, but we experience the world as a set of dualities, dichotomies, dilemmas and ambiguities. The drive to unity is thus an imperative made all the more demanding by the basic schism that underlies experience. Both the 'drive', and the original schism that is the source of our dualistic view of life, transcend, or lie upstream of, the conscious mind. Even so, the effect of the drive to unity is evident in all that we do. Our search for the holy in religion, for truth in philosophy, for harmony in relations with others, our search for certainty in science, as well as much of what is done in the corporate world, come from the same drive to unity. Ironically, dualistic on/off logic also comes from this same drive to unity. The basic principle of this logic, the principle of identity or oneness, derives it power to convince from the drive to unity. Failure to find unity in a conflicting dissonant situation can arouse feelings of profound insecurity, anxiety, anguish and stress.

An important guiding principle in scientific research is Occam's razor, which says that unproven assumptions must be reduced to a minimum. Occam's razor is the principle of simplicity and the word 'simple' comes from the root word *sem* which means 'one.' At the same time some scientists are inspired by a search for an all-inclusive theory, a theory of everything. Moreover, we feel ourselves to be 'individuals', that which is one and cannot be divided, yet see the world as a 'universe', a word that originally means 'return to the one'. So, although dynamic unity cannot be perceived or intellectually grasped in a meaningful way, we can see that its effects pervade nature and human experience.

What does it mean to think?

I remember when I was in early grade school and the teacher shouted at us, "You must think! You are not thinking!" I had no idea what she meant. How does one think? I would squeeze my eyes shut and hope that somehow this was what she meant, that somehow something would pop out. The word 'think' was inscribed on small panels that IBM managers placed on their desks. They may still do this. If a company as illustrious as IBM insists on thinking then thinking must have real value. But, what does 'to think' mean? Later, when I was studying for a degree in philosophy, I was taught classical logic and the different syllogisms and I thought, "Ah! at last I know how to think." But it was not long before I realized that the process of thinking was far, far more complicated than the rules of logic seemed to indicate. In fact, I did not think at all in the way the text books seemed to say that I should think!

Artificial Intelligence research scientists believe that they can create machines that will think. Some have claimed that these machines will think a great deal more efficiently than human beings do. Even so, in more recent years some have come to realize that the human mind is much more complex than they had formerly believed. Perception, creativity and thinking are inextricably mixed; the mind does not just process information, it also creates and organizes it in the very act of perceiving it. Memory and emotions are essential elements in this creative process. While it is true that some thinking has been formalized, formal or logical thinking is only used in its pure form in some specific and very limited cases in mathematics, scientific research and, perhaps more frequently, in philosophic thought.

I have so far identified two ways that the mind works: creatively and logically. These two ways are intimately connected because a creative situation has at least two incompatible frames of reference and classical logic is the logic of incompatibility: either something is the case or it is not. While classical logic, by its very nature, has to choose the either/or way of thinking as the only real way to think, creative thinking does not have to dismiss classical logic but uses it to identify the incompatible frames of reference and then goes beyond them.

Creative and logical thinking are ways by which we deal with the underlying schism of the mind, and so bring order into experience. Between these two extremes, many other levels and nuances of mental activity are possible. Moreover, emotions and feelings, including the feelings of tension and stress, are inextricably mingled with cognitive activities.

I will discuss briefly some of the other levels. For the sake of convenience I have ranged mental activities into a spectrum with creativity at the top and logical thinking at the bottom of the scale, although our subjective world is usually just confused and disorderly. The spectrum will help avoid thinking simplistically about the mind; that is to say, thinking that the mind is simply an information processing system. It will also help us to appreciate the nuances of mental activity and perhaps to have a better understanding of others and ourselves.

The drive to divide the world logically into either/or gets its momentum from the deep schism or wound in our being. Using the principle of identity [1] we are able to see the world as one, and so get beyond haunting fear, anxiety and stress, and even feel a measure of security and certainty. But to achieve security we must divide our experience of the world in two, and then dispense with one half. This is the strategy of materialism when faced with the mind/body dilemma. But the materialist strategy of rejecting half the situation cannot always be used. So other strategies become necessary for palliating the inner wound, and coping with the contradictions that are inherent to our nature. I list some of these in the spectrum. Let me describe its different levels, and then later I will delve more deeply into the implications that our doing so has for understanding a company and work.

The spectrum

During the following discussion I will simply state the conflict as Yes and No, but Yes/No will also stand for good/bad, right/wrong, me/you, manager/worker, and all the other dualities, dichotomies or divisions that are encountered in experience. Please remember that these dualities are ultimately based upon, because they arise out of, the primary ambiguity or schism that I wrote about in chapter one. Thought, perception and creativity are ways that we have acquired through long centuries of acculturation to come to terms with such an impossible contradiction.

Creativity	YES and NO happily married
Ambiguity	YES as NO NO as Yes
Dilemma	Both YES and NO but either YES or NO
Frustration	Its gotta be YES or NO!
Compromise	Both YES and NO

Complementary	Both YES and NO
Anger	YES! (Or NO!)
Dogma and morality	Assert YES over NO
Worry and anxiety	Cannot resolve YES or NO
More or less	From YES to NO From NO to YES
Logical	YES or No

Logical or on/off thinking

I have already discussed this at some length and will not add anything further.

More or less thinking

Not all light switches are of the 'on or off' variety. Dimmer switches are also available and when used the light is more or less 'on' or 'off'. A dimmer switch allows a gradient from 'barely on' to 'fully on'. Occasionally the mind also thinks in this way. For example, if someone were to ask whether you are going out tonight you might answer 'possibly' or perhaps 'probably'. Both 'possibly' and 'probably' appear somewhere along a 'yes/no' gradient, with 'possibly' being nearer to the 'no' and 'probably' nearer to the 'yes'. Such thinking moreover is flexible: 'possibly' can easily turn into 'probably' and 'probably' turn again into 'possibly' depending on the circumstances. In order that we can refer to it again later, let us call it *more or less thinking*. This type of thinking is used when we mull over a problem. Computers, with what are called neuro-logical networks or fields, have simulated more or less thinking. Logical thought simply cuts the basic contradiction into two and discards one or other half. More or less thinking comes from an inability or unwillingness to do this.

Worry or anxiety

Worrying is thinking accompanied by a feeling of confusion, uncertainty, anxiety and indecision. Whereas on/off thinking is certain and clear-cut, and more or less thinking smooth and flexible, worry is neither the one nor the other since it is neither clear nor flexible. Or, one could also say it is both 'on/off' and 'more or less' thinking, since it has the rigidity of 'on/off' thinking, and the uncertainty of 'more or less' thinking.

With worry we cannot settle on yes or no but the drive to unity compels us to do so. No sooner do we settle on 'yes' than 'no' offers itself. If we then settle on 'no,' then 'yes' starts intruding and we wonder whether 'no' is the answer after all. A feeling of pervasive anguish and insecurity accompanies such mental activity. Everyone knows this mind state. I have a pain in the side; I wonder "Is it serious?" I decide it is and make up my mind to see a doctor. Then I wonder whether it really is all that serious and decide not to go. The pain persists: I think I will go. What if it really is serious? I think that I will wait . . . and so on back and forth. The pain and anguish that underlies worry and anxiety do not come from the reasons that we give for anxiety, but from the basic wound, the tear in unity that the worrying exposes.

Worry and anxiety can become intolerable. Because of them the stable point that we call 'I' is losing its stability, and the underlying basic contradiction begins to wake up and make itself known. We then begin to be anxious about anxiety. Then we begin to panic about the anxiety and then panic because we are panicking. We get caught up in a vortex of anguish. Other negative emotions also can have a spiraling nature. We are depressed then depressed about depression, then depressed about that. One reason why some people cling so grimly at all costs to logical thinking is to stave off the threat of ultimate instability, which they perceive as a loss of control.

Morality thinking

Another kind thinking is *morality* thinking: I *ought* to do this, I *must* do that, I *should* do something else. Another name for morality thinking could be *ought* thinking, thinking which asserts good over bad. Let us make a distinction between moral thinking and ethical thinking. Moral thinking is based upon fixed rules called moral codes, and these are given in terms of black or white, 'thou shalt' and 'thou shalt not'. Ethical conduct on the other hand is thinking that is sensitive to the nuances of the situation. Such sensitivity comes out of a high tolerance for ambiguity and a keen awareness of wholeness and unity. 'Must', 'ought', 'should', all of these give expression to the categorical imperative of *Let there be One!* Ethical thinking arises from the recognition of the One (or the whole).

Most often moral or ought thinking is a buffer against the threat of uncertainty, indecision and anxiety. The rise of fundamentalism in the Islamic societies is partly due to the social upheavals that technology is inflicting on developing countries and the severe stress that this arouses in the people in those countries. The support for the far right in America comes from similar fears and concerns. The moral is associated with good, but that this is not necessarily so is shown by the activity of terrorists and by the extreme intolerance of some of the 'moral majority', both groups feel that they act in the name of the good and the righteous. This is why I have called it ought thinking as well as moral thinking. Nazi Germany was ruled by the 'ought', or so-called iron will, of Hitler and few people now would call that regime good.

A further distinction yet deserves to be made and that is to distinguish between moral thinking and legal thinking. Many executives in corporations believe that as long as they stay within the law they may do as they please. Relying on the law in this way relieves the executive of the burden that both moral and ethical thinking bring with them.

Anger

Anger is one of the ways we use the mind to mitigate the effects of the deep split that lies at the heart of our being; it is an extreme reaction to the uncertainty and pain that the split can induce. Anger violently asserts 'yes' over 'no', or 'no' over 'yes,' and it will often be found to be the other side of anxiety. The anguish of uncertainty can get so great that some resolution *must* be found. If no rules are available, then anger or even violence is a forceful way of breaking the deadlock. They are ways of trying to ram home an unequivocal, stable point. Anger and moral thinking can often be found together.

Complementarity

Night and day, nut and bolt, inside and outside of a cup, are complementaries. Complementaries complete each other within a given whole. Physics has encountered many complementaries that seem to be rooted in reality itself. Possibly the most well known illustration of complementaries is the Chinese symbol for Yin and Yang

The theoretical physicist Neils Bohr, who contributed greatly to the advances in quantum physics, used complementary thinking to account for the anomaly of the wave/particle that occurred in research at a sub atomic level: when certain experiments were conducted a photon would behave as a particle, when other experiments were conducted it would behave as a wave. That his coat of arms included the above symbol shows the extent to which his thinking was pervaded by complementaries. Complementary thinking looks beyond the duality to the Unity on which they are founded.

Figure 5.1 Yin Yang: complementarity

Although they are similar, complementary thinking and the logic of ambiguity are also profoundly different. Whereas logical thinking declares, *either* YES or NO, complementary thinking affirms, *both* YES and NO. Ambiguity, on the other hand, says, *either* YES or NO and *both* YES and NO.

Compromise

Compromise is closely associated with complementary thinking. Compromise, like complementary thinking, is a way to maintain unity or harmony. Whereas in complementary thinking both YES and NO are left intact, with compromise both YES and NO are equally diminished in some way.

Frustration

Frustration is a common enough experience. As a rule it is accompanied by an acute tension and feeling of being paralyzed in some way. Someone said that it is like a rat in a bamboo tube: it cannot go forward; it cannot retreat but cannot stay where it is. I cannot say 'yes', cannot say 'no', and 'maybe' is unacceptable.

Dilemma

Although I have already written about dilemma, nevertheless let me say a little more. With a dilemma there are at least two, although sometimes more, ways of acting in response to a situation. Only one of these ways can be chosen and acted upon at any given time, although both ways are equally good or desirable — or both equally bad and undesirable. In other words, at some particular time *to do the right thing is to do the wrong thing*, which is to reject the right thing. Let me give you a very topical and pressing dilemma that society is faced with.

Should a woman have the right to an abortion if and when she wishes? Some say, "Yes! It is her body, and no one has the right to dictate what she should or should not do with her body." As we know, these people hold onto their point of view with passion. Others say, "No!" because she would be destroying life and 'Thou shalt not kill' is an imperative that has justifiably been acknowledged by the great religions. Again these people hold onto their view with great passion.

Now, for some people both alternatives have equal weight. Therefore for such people to do the right thing — in this instance allow the woman to do as she pleases with her body — is to do the wrong thing — stand by and doing nothing while life is destroyed. The opposite is also true. If I say a woman should not be allowed to have an abortion, then I agree that some arbitrary power should be able to decree what a woman should do with her body.

This is like the story of a judge who, having heard the counsel for the defense, turned to him and said, "Yes! You are right!" Then the counsel for the prosecution stood and said his piece. Again the judge turned to him and said, "Yes! You are right!" Then the clerk of the court, hot under the collar, leapt up and exclaimed, "But, m'lud, they both can't be right," and the judge turned to him and said, "Yes! You are right!"

On/off thinking demands either a 'yes' or 'no': yes, a woman should be the one to decide to carry the baby; or no, she does not have this right. With a dilemma one cannot say yes or no, because both courses of action are right, or both are wrong. However, what distinguishes a dilemma from an ambiguity is that when one is faced by a dilemma one *must* respond. Not to respond is itself a response. One must find an answer; one must make a decision. One *cannot* say either yes or no, but one *must* say either yes or no. A manager is constantly confronted with dilemmas, and these contribute to the burden of management.

I said that worry is a hybrid bred from 'on/off,' and 'more or less' thinking. Now we can see a third ingredient of worry: the dilemma. On/off thinking assumes either one alternative or the other must be the right one; dilemma thinking keeps coming up with two equally acceptable alternatives. Worry just goes back and forth, from one horn of the dilemma to the other and back. Worry is similar to 'more or less' thinking, but different since it cannot rest, it is always on the move. "If I allow my daughter to continue to go out with the crowd she's with, she'll land up in trouble. But on the other hand, if I don't let her choose her own friends how will she ever stand on her own feet?" If you are a parent, this type of situation will surely sound familiar to you. Anger is a way to crash through the roadblock.

'Ought' thinking, like worry, is also a hybrid; but this time, instead of worrying about the problem and constantly going back and forth between the two alternatives, we simply refuse to entertain one or the other of them. "No, she cannot go out with that crowd because it is wrong!" The refusal is dogmatic, even though the dilemma keeps demanding both alternatives be entertained. The rejected or ignored alternative does not go away. It keeps pressing for its own resolution. The need to overcome such pressure accounts for the force many people need to back up moral and dogmatic thinking, and to contain the potentially explosive situation that it creates, a situation that can and sometimes does end in anger and rage.

Are we then condemned to oscillate permanently through these alternatives except when, on those very rare occasions in life, we can make a clear choice of yes or no? The way out may well be found in creativity. However, before talking about that let me say something more about ambiguity, which has so much in common with dilemma.

Ambiguity

Although everyone knows about ambiguity, its importance in conscious life is often overlooked, except in the realm of the arts. Poetry, music, architecture, painting, really all the arts, when they are authentic, have ambiguity as a basic ingredient.[2] Beethoven said music is a higher revelation than science. In so far as the spirit of music dwells in ambiguity while that of science dwells in 'either/or' thinking, then Beethoven is right, although in the end they both equally demand creativity. Ambiguity is also at the root of authentic mystical and spiritual life. In corporate life, too, we live and work in a very ambiguous domain and when called upon to act we are often faced with dilemmas.

Creativity

I have put creativity at the top of the spectrum because all the rest of the spectrum is derived from it. Creativity is the original way that life resolves the dilemma and creativity has ambiguity as its basis. Creativity achieves harmony between two points of view which are interdependent, but which are incompatible and so exclude each other. The impossibility, either A or B/both A and B, is resolved in an entirely original way. The resolution is arrived at without sacrificing either A or B.

People who used a certain very high building complained because the elevators were too slow. Nevertheless to install more or faster elevators would have been too costly. The owners were faced with a cost/quality dilemma. They had to do something because people tended to avoid the building as they did not like waiting, and that meant loss of customers. So what should the owners do? They had both to keep the customers and to keep the costs down. But either they had to lose customers or let the costs rise. Some bright person said, "Give the people something interesting to do while they wait." But what? Then another came up with the solution: install mirrors. Everyone likes looking at themselves in a mirror, as well as looking at other people looking at themselves in the mirror. By installing mirrors the tedium of waiting could be overcome with the least cost.

I shall be returning to creativity, ambiguity and dilemma repeatedly and will show that they have many different guises. The importance of creativity becomes obvious when it is remembered that life is based upon a fundamental ambiguity. Indeed a case could be made for saying that all civilizations come from, and evolve out of, the urge to find some resolution of this ambiguity.

Additions to the spectrum

The spectrum is by no means complete and is only offered to give an idea of the influence of the deep split that rends us in the heart of our being and so modifies all experience. For example, I could have included *pretending* in the spectrum. Pretence is making believe that it is YES when really it is NO (or NO when it is YES). A child playing with a doll pretends the doll is alive, knowing all the while that it is not. *Judging* is comparing YES with NO, which is what a trial judge has to do. *Deceiving* is saying YES knowing we should say NO. "Did you spill milk all over the floor?" "No, it must have been the cat." (But it was you all the time.) *Denying* is refusing to accept YES and asserting NO instead. Kubler-Ross who introduced the five stages in the dying process said that denial was one of these stages. The patient knows she is going to die but says NO I am not! *Hypocrisy* is when your boss comes up with his usual banal statements and you tell him what an interesting guy he is. *Two-timer, two faced* are ways of talking about a hypocrite. We talk about being between a rock and a hard place, meaning we are faced with YES and NO and cannot but must make a decision.

To sum up

Corporations are rooted in the creativity of human beings. Indeed they could be seen as extensions of the human mind and human creativity. To understand a corporation, and in particular the organization of a corporation, we have to have some understanding of human nature. The division or wound at the very heart of our being causes stress and suffering, but nevertheless is also the source of creativity. Our basic creation is our identity or the sense of self that we call 'I'. The more stable and secure is this sense of self , the more secure I feel. 'I' is invested in many different situations. Possibly the most important of these for the modern Westerner is the work that he or she does.

The basic drive in life is provided by dynamic unity, which in human beings is expressed as will, intention, commitment, drive and ambition. It is also the drive that powers competitiveness, the will to win, to dominate, and to triumph, both in us and in the institutions that we create. The same dynamic unity compels us to seek pattern, structure, order and organization. The most primitive way this is done is through perception.

Work, creativity, and conflict share the same basic pattern. I used the word isomorphic to designate the similarity of pattern. The implication of this is that work, which is a way we give form to the creative impulse, is a fundamental need in a human being, as fundamental as sex, food and shelter. Furthermore, conflict, which comes in the form of dilemmas and ambiguity, is a necessary aspect of both work and creativity. The effort to overcome the tension involved in the conflict brought about by dilemmas is what makes mental work hard.

The way that we have been taught to think inhibits creativity. Logical thinking encourages us to divide a dilemma and to believe that only one of its faces is legitimate, which means that we reject many of the difficulties that we should be dealing with. Although they are ignored or suppressed, these difficulties do not go away but return in a different guise and all the more demanding of attention. Logical thought not only inhibits creativity, it also makes ethical behavior very difficult as it forces us back onto moral behavior, which in corporate life may be interpreted simply as staying within the law. I have therefore suggested a new logic: the logic of ambiguity. Using it managers can become sensitive to the whole situation and to its nuances, and so are enabled to make ethical decisions.

This final chapter of Part One has been devoted to showing how complex the mind is when dealing with the difficulties of life. However, it has also been written to show that this vast complexity could be understood as the reaction to the basic contradiction that lies at our heart.

The first part of the book has given us a firm ground on which to stand to begin exploring a company and its organization, and during this exploration we will see the themes of dynamic unity, ambiguity, dilemma and conflict, in the form of commitment and intention, creativity and work, played out in a variety of ways.

The first step in the exploration will be to delve more deeply into the meaning of the word work, because work sustains a company and maintains the mental health of us all.

Notes

1   x = x.
2   Leonard Bernstein gives a wonderful exposition of the role of ambiguity in music in his Charles Eliot Norton lectures at Harvard in 1973. See Leonard Bernstein, *The Unanswered Question: Six talks at Harvard* (Cambridge, MA: Harvard University Press, 1976).

PART TWO

The Structure of Work

CHAPTER SIX

Work and Organization

The importance of work

Let us start by talking more specifically about work, which of course includes *employment* work. By 'employment' work I mean the work that we do to earn a living. Most of us spend much of our adult life at work in some kind of institution, and, although earning money is an important reason for doing so, we also work to satisfy, among other needs, the needs to be creative, to belong and to contribute. If you have ever been laid off and unable to find work for a while, you will know how debilitating the experience can be. One loses self-respect, loses energy and the will to do, and one has a pervasive feeling of humiliation and guilt. Not only is the need to work a part of our being, but our very identity, the sense of whom and what we are, is closely tied into work. How often does one ask, when talking to a stranger, "What do you do?" meaning, "What is your work?" By doing so one places him or her into the context of society as a whole.[1]

The fact that someone will pay me for the work that I do gives additional value to that activity, I feel that I am 'worth something'. Van Gogh, when he was unemployed and before he became a painter, cried out in a letter to his brother, Theo, that he, van Gogh, was one of those people, "who are somehow mysteriously imprisoned, prisoners in an I-don't-know-what-for horrible, horrible, utterly horrible cage. Such a man often does not know himself what he might do but feels instinctively: yet I am good for something . . . How then can I be useful, how can I be of service! Something is alive in me: what can it be?"[2] Such could be the cry of any unemployed person.

A company comes into being because of work, is sustained by work, and expands and grows with work. If the basic aims of a company are to survive and to contribute to society, these aims are realized through work. The way work is done, and how well it is done, sustains the company's health, as well as the health, mental and physical, of the employees. The less efficiently a company produces its product — that is, the less effective its organization is — the poorer the organizational health and the weaker its constitution. The inefficiency of the company will in turn feed back onto the employees through badly structured assignments and less interesting challenge, and their well-being will decline accordingly.

To understand a company organization, one must understand work, and while doing so one must keep in mind the dual value of work: the value it has for each of us, and the value it has for the company. Furthermore, because the greater part of a country's adult population is at work, we are talking about the mental health and general state of well-being of most of the population.

A more detailed definition of work

Even though work plays such an important part in life, the word 'work' has only recently been adequately defined. Before then managers did not know in a conscious way the meaning of the word work. Even now most have a hard time saying what they mean by the word. I have asked many managers how they understand it. They have replied, 'physical exertion', 'spending time doing things', 'putting out mental effort', 'something that is done to get some worthwhile result', or 'putting things together'. The physicist's clear definition of work as the force times the distance through which the force acts stands in stark contrast to the poorly organized thinking that occurs about what is so important in giving meaning and structure to our lives. Such a lack of a clear definition makes it difficult to think or talk about work in a clear and precise way, which in turn makes it likely that any discussion about company organization, including the organization of work, will end in confusion.

When most people think about work they think of something unpleasant, of something hard, perhaps of something from which to escape if possible. The French word for work is *travail*, which is derived from the Latin *tripalium*, an instrument of torture. Even those who enjoy work would agree that often doing it is quite hard. Working is hard not because physical energy is expended — many people find mental work much harder than physical work and will be even more ready to avoid it — but because of the struggle with ambiguities and dilemmas. Unable to sustain the mental effort required, many will be found walking around the office building, signing forms, fiddling with the computer, entering into discussions, attending meetings: in fact, doing anything but mental work.

In chapter three I defined work as the exercise of discretion within limits to produce a result, and showed the connection that work has with creativity. Creativity, according to Koestler, is a single idea in two *incompatible* frames of reference. Work and creativity are isomorphic because the limits within which work is done are incompatible. I shall later give many examples of incompatibility that are met with when doing work. Work that is done to overcome, and so go beyond incompatibility, necessarily has elements of conflict, tension and stress. Logically the limits are restrictions; creatively they are resources. But to make a transition from restriction to resources through creativity, the worker has to bear the burden of the tension created by the incompatibility of the limits.

Work is done to produce a result. Activity that produces no result is nothing more than activity. It is not work. Later I shall refine what I mean by a result. For the moment it is enough to say that one must concentrate one's mind and energies to produce it, and the effort that such concentration demands also adds another reason for saying that work is hard.

Although limits are imposed upon activity at work, and the need to produce a result concentrates one's energies, nevertheless at any level in an organization one is expected to exercise *discretion* within those limits. As I am simply giving an overview, I'll leave open for the moment a precise meaning of the word 'discretion'. Let me just call it 'know-how'; later I will explore it in detail and define it more clearly.

Finally one expects to get paid to do the work

Work can, therefore, be defined as the application of discretion within limits in order to produce a result. To give the full definition proposed by Elliott Jaques who was the first to define work thus: *Employment work is the application of knowledge and the exercise of discretion within limits prescribed by the immediate manager and by higher policies, in order to carry out the activities allocated by the immediate manager, the whole carried out within an employment contract for a wage or salary.*[3]

The importance of limits

No one in a company, from the CEO down, is able to do as he or she likes. Limits are imposed on people at all levels and in all parts of a company. To do work we need limits. Without limits we could not work. Many people are of the opinion that freedom lies in the absence of limits, an opinion shared by some modern artists who feel that artistic freedom is to have no limits, to be unrestrained. Limits are important because they contain our creative energies.

The work generated by an internal combustion engine can serve as a metaphor. The cylinder walls are the limits, the compressed gas is the means, and the moving piston that turns a shaft is the result. The more perfectly the walls are adjusted to contain the gas, the more efficient the operation will be. If the walls of the cylinder do not fit the piston tightly enough, gas escapes and efficiency suffers. If the cylinder fits the piston too tightly, energy is wasted through friction, heat, and noise. Nevertheless the cylinder is necessary for the piston to do its work.

The limits of work performed in a company have a further interest because they have a recognizable structure that is repeated at all levels within a company, from the simplest function to the president of the company. This structure expresses itself in different ways, but is basically the same structure, and therefore any job in a company is *isomorphic* with any other job.

Isomorphisms are recurring shapes or patterns. One of the most important ingredients in understanding is *pattern*. Identifying a pattern that is similar in a number of different systems is a basis for intelligent behavior. Isomorphisms simplify the way we think. Mathematics, which is the basis for so much of our understanding, has been called the science of pattern, and much of scientific research is the search for pattern. Patterns of behavior in the physical world are called laws. When we can find recurring patterns within a company organization our understanding of the organization will become that much greater. Moreover by identifying a number of systems that are isomorphic, the solutions arrived at when solving the problems of one system may well be useful in solving problems that arise in other systems. The basic pattern of a job that I shall identify is the same pattern as that which underlies the creative process.

The definition of work applied to the work of a filing assistant

To see what the limits of work are, consider the simplest level of work such as that of a filing assistant. Filing has been made redundant in many companies by the widespread use of computers. Even so some institutions still employ men or women to file documents, for example patients' medical records in a hospital. From such an example the importance of limits and why they are incompatible will be made clearer.

Let us suppose that a filing assistant is required to put reports, test results, documents, and other material into an existing system according to a specified code. The assistant is given the material daily in a random order and he must file each day's quota that day or else fall behind in his work. Let us then ask what limits are involved? Another way of asking the question is, "How are we to judge how well the assistant does his work?" Two criteria present themselves: (1) has the assistant filed the material according to the code? The degree to which he follows the code gives his work a certain degree of *quality*. (2) Was the work done in the time allowed? I have said that each day's quota must be filed that day and so we can assess the work by asking whether the assistant has completed his quota. Thus, the two limits of a filing assistant's job are *quality* and *pace*, and the filing assistant is in a position to trade one limit against the other and so accomplish the work. If he speeds up the work the possibility of making mistakes increases. If he spends more time ensuring that the code is followed, then he works slower and may fall behind. The limits are therefore ultimately incompatible.

We can determine whether work or mere activity is involved by simply asking whether discretion is allowed within limits. If no discretion is allowed, if the limits are so restrictive that the assistant has no freedom to choose between alternatives, then activity, but not work, is involved. As an illustration, let us compare the work of a filing assistant with the work of someone working on a conveyor belt who is given a wrench that is so constructed that only a given pressure can be applied to a nut. Such a worker is unable to trade time against quality as both are fixed: the conveyor sets the time; the spanner determines the quality. His discretion is so limited that it could be considered as an activity but not work as I have defined it. The inventive genius of production engineers has for years been devoted to designing just this sort of activity. An example of work that requires the bare minimum of discretion is the work of a checkout assistant in a super-market.

Multi-task jobs

A filing assistant is doing what could be called a *single task job*. But an employee is rarely just given one single task to perform. More often jobs are *multitask* jobs, that is, they require more than one task cycle to be completed. Often typing, answering the telephone, mailing letters, and other tasks may be allocated to go along with filing tasks.

In such a multi-task job the assistant is required to organize a system of machines, equipment, paper, and knowledge; that is, to bring these together not only within the limits of pace and quality but also according to priorities. The introduction of priorities therefore creates a new limit and a new dimension to work appears.

At a higher level still, say first line supervision, the 'quality' limits of the job will also include standard practices, policies and procedures. The pace limit will include a discretionary budget or discretionary expenditure as an added dimension. Priority will be the third limit, but priorities

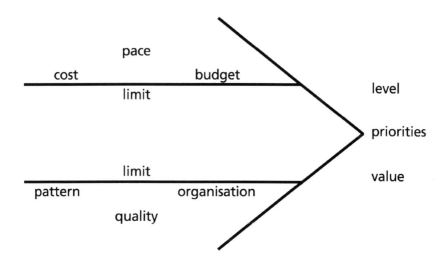

Figure 6.1 Work

will be set, not just by the dictates of getting a variety of different kinds of work done, but also by assigning work to subordinates.

Cost-pattern-level

Quality and organization both have pattern, structure or inner interrelationship in common. For example, the filing assistant has a filing system, an organized set of records that he is adding to each day. He is required to maintain the integrity of the system and the extent to which he does so will determine the quality of the work that he does. A supervisor of a group of technical personnel has a system of people that he must organized in such a way that they are assigned work in the most efficient way. An executive of a department has the organization of the department. I shall be going deeper into what I mean by 'organizing a department' in the third part of the book. The essential thing is that one limit has inherently a structure that requires constant maintenance.

'Pace' refers to the time required to reach a result. The time allowance for the filing assistant was one day. The time allowed a V.P. of Marketing to introduce a new marketing plan might well be a year or more depending on the circumstances. The time allowance for the filing assistant is explicit, the time allowance for the V.P. may well be implicit, yet nevertheless it would have to fit in with the overall time frame within which his company is operating.

Time and cost are intimately connected. For example, the filing assistant may get a pre-sorting machine to help sort the documents before filing. The costs are increased but more is accomplished in the time allowed. When I was young, about nine men wielding 14 lb sledge-hammers for a couple of hours were needed to break up the pavement to repair a gas leak. They would stand in a circle and in unison hit a chisel, often chanting as they worked. Now, with pneumatic jackham-mers attached to a backhoe it takes one man a few minutes. Thus the budget of a manager is associated with the pace limit of the filing assis-tant. This bears out the old adage that time is money.

Most managers have a budget within which to operate. The more fortunate have an explicit budget, the less fortunate, an implicit one. A manager with an implicit budget is like a man who is asked to go to a wall with his eyes closed. He knows the wall is there, but he has to exer-cise a fair degree of caution in reaching it.

The priority limit of the filing assistant would simply be determined by the sequence he followed when filing the documents; that is to say he would decide which should be filed first, second and so on. A manager on the other hand would have to set priorities for himself and for the people working for him. His own priorities would also be influ-enced by the need to ensure that the work of his department gets done in time, and also the need to ensure that the integrity of his department was maintained. Priorities furthermore are normally ranged in a scale with the most important put at the top of the scale. Thus level, priority and value make up the third limit.

A common structure of cost-pattern-level governs all work and the jobs of a company are all isomorphic.

Managerial and technical work

Management science is, in the main, based upon the assumption that a manager is called upon to solve problems. I am suggesting that while true, this does not tell the whole story. Any job has a *technical* dimen-sion and a *managerial* dimension. The proportion of time spent on each will change as one ascends the hierarchy — less time will be spent on technical work and more on managerial. With technical work a right answer is possible. With managerial work a 'right' answer cannot be found because as well as coping with problems, a manager is called upon to work with dilemmas. I spoke about this in chapter three when I discussed creativity, choice and calculation. Thus when I use the term *manager* I will normally mean the *managerial or discretionary* aspect, and so the job of a filing assistant has a 'managerial' that is to say, discre-tionary, aspect.

The cost/quality dilemma that I have been describing, also known as the cost/benefit dilemma, is just one among the many dilemmas that pervade work. All of these have the baffling characteristic that while I have to satisfy the demands of both horns of the dilemma at the same time, I can only satisfy the demands of one: and yet I reject one or the other at my peril. I can oscillate between the two alternatives and never come to a decision. Such an oscillation approximates the solution arrived at by Bruno's ass: fixed exactly midway between two bales of hay it starved to death. Many managers, aware at some level of the dilemma, and wanting the best of both worlds, are unwilling to relinquish either horn but are unable to realize both and so they end up with neither.

Common dilemmas

The following are among the more common dilemmas

Process	Structure
Individual	System
Urgent	Important
Cost	Quality (Benefit)
Function	Product
Risk	Waste
Expression	Survival

Normally the two horns of the dilemma can be satisfied by alternating between them, addressing now one, now the other, or by balancing the demands of each by allocating resources in an equitable way. For the latter course of action to be possible, management must recognize that these dilemmas do arise and so create in advance an adequate organization with proper allocation of resources so that the necessary steps can be taken to satisfy the two horns of the dilemma. When such an organization is not created, both horns will be presented simultaneously and some creative decisions must be made.

Each of the dilemmas is discussed below.

Structure/Process

Peter Drucker has said, "Each organization has the task of balancing the need for order against the need for flexibility and individual scope. Each requires a structure determined by 'generic principles of organization,' that is, in effect, by constitutional rules."[4] He goes on to state the dilemma by asking whether the structure should be absolute and according to the principles of organization or whether it should be focused on specific objectives and strategy and so tailored to meet the logic of the situation. In other words, should it be tailored toward structure or process.

System/Individual

The system/individual dilemma is encountered fairly frequently. The following is an example: An employee requests time off with pay because her aunt has died. The personnel policy states that time off with pay is permitted when an immediate member of the family has died. The definition in the policy of 'immediate family' does not include an aunt. In this example, the personnel policy represents the system; the employee requesting time off represents the individual. On the face of it no problem exists. The answer is quite clear. The personnel policy does not allow a person to take time off with pay in order to mourn the death of an aunt.

The employee points out though that her mother died when she was very young and the aunt has fulfilled the role of mother for her throughout her life. The personnel policy did not envisage such a relationship so the manager has a dilemma. If he accedes to the request, the system suffers; if the request is denied, the individual suffers. The system would suffer because if the employee were allowed time off with pay, the clarity of definition that the policy once had, and needs to have to be effective as a guide, would be diminished. The individual would suffer if not given time off because she will not have the time to mourn the death of one she loved.

Urgent/Important

An interesting example of the urgent/important dilemma occurred during World War II. Later model Spitfires were equipped with a special boosting device on the throttle. The pilot was able to increase the speed of the aircraft in an emergency by pushing the throttle through a 'gate'. If he did so he increased the wear and tear on the aircraft considerably. The pilot was warned against using the booster for more than a specified time. If the booster were used for longer than specified, the vibrations could shake the engine off its mounting and the whole frame of the aircraft would be threatened. Thus, in combat, the pilot could be faced with the dilemma: urgent/important. Urgent: the enemy is bearing down with blazing guns! Important: the engine and the aircraft must be kept serviceable in order to get home and, where possible, fly again!

Urgent problems have specified time limits that can be known, the outcome is uncertain, but the problem is obvious. With an important problem, on the other hand, the outcome is certain, the time unknown, and the problem hidden. Many people tend to feel that the urgent problem is a practical one, whereas the important problem is 'theoretical'. A crisis could be said to arise when the important problem becomes urgent. Most frequently urgent work takes precedence over important work. One should not be surprised, therefore, at the fact that crises often have to be precipitated in order to get important things done.

The following is an example of a fairly typical important/urgent dilemma. You must have enough gas in the your car to get where you want to go; this is important. But suppose that to get enough gas you have to make a fairly long detour and you have an appointment to keep. If you go to get the gas you will be late. That you arrive on time is urgent, but if you do not get the gas you may not arrive at all.

Cost/Quality

I have already dealt with the cost/quality dilemma. A manager frequently expresses it in the questions, "How much quality do I sacrifice to save costs?" or, "How much do I increase my costs in order to have the extra quality that will give me the margin over my competitors?" Many managers will know the dilemma as a cost/benefit dilemma.

Waste/Risk

Managers are not so familiar with the waste/risk dilemma because they are more oriented toward the risk pole rather than the waste. Most managers recognize that they face risks in much of what they do, but strangely few recognize the problem of waste. Using other words, management seems generally aware of the sin of commission but generally unaware of the sin of omission. The problem of waste and the burden created by it is often carried unconsciously and, because it is unconscious, the burden is all that more irksome. The sin of omission may occur when a manager decides to do nothing rather than take a risk, even though deciding to do nothing is still a decision although often an unconscious one. By deciding to do nothing a manager may waste a valuable opportunity.

A market may exist for a modification of the product that the manager is employed to produce. It's a risk to modify the product, should he take it? He says, "Let's wait for a while and see." His competitor produces the modified product and takes the market.

The waste/risk dilemma can be understood in another way. Time must be given to developing a product, to designing it, to planning production, to ensuring that sales staff will be trained, and to getting everyone onboard who will be involved in producing and selling the product. If these steps are not taken, then later, after production has begun, difficulties that should have been anticipated in the planning and development stage may well arise and slow down the process and so risk losing time, resources and even the contract. On the other hand if too much time is given to the planning stage, then time could be wasted in fruitless discussion, endless recycling of ideas and a loss of momentum. If inadequate product development is undertaken, then the risk is considerably increased. If, on the other hand, the product development phase is increased out of proportion to the other phase, then the likelihood of waste is increased.

A specific example of waste and risk occurs when you go on a journey by car to somewhere you have never been before. To prepare adequately you should consult maps and be sure that the proposed route is the best available. Quite possibly the time you spend on consulting the map may be wasted; the road conditions may be such that the route selected turns out to be impossible. Therefore, many people object to setting up plans, or, rather, undertaking product-development work. They say that no one can be sure that the situation will not have changed by the time the project is to be implemented.

Without consulting the map, however, you are constantly faced with the risk that the route you are taking will go through the most difficult terrain, or even in the wrong direction. Without a plan the situations that arise can only be dealt with on an ad hoc basis, and progress in the present may be bought at the expense of progress in the future.

The Japanese have a very keen sense of the product development phase. Many Americans doing business with them feel that for some time the Japanese are simply wasting time. But the most important factor in decision making for the Japanese is to find the question. This necessarily leads to the question whether a need for a decision exists and if so what the decision is about. All of this takes a long time of course. The Westerner is likely to be frustrated, because for him answers are what matter.

Product/Function

The product/function dilemma is a perennial one in organization. Should work be delegated according to the product being produced or to the function being performed? "The dilemma of product versus function is by no means new; managers have been facing the same basic question for decades. Corporations, especially manufacturers, have long wrestled with the problem of how to structure their organizations to enable employees, particularly specialists, to do their jobs with maximum efficiency and productivity. One perplexing issue has been whether to organize around functions or products. The question is whether specialists in a given function should be grouped under a common boss, regardless of the differences in products they are involved in, or should the various functional specialists, working on a single product, be grouped together under the same superior."[5]

Those who argue in favor of organization by function say that such an organization enables the best use to be made of up-to-date technical skills as well as making it possible to ensure the most effective division of labor and specialization. Furthermore, when organizing by function, better use is made of labor saving devices and mass-production.

Those who argue for organization by product will say that it provides a better basis for integration and co-ordination. The employees are more involved in the total product, and the work they do is more enriching. This will likely create greater challenge as the work is more personalized, calling forth greater commitment.

A writer on management theory, J. W. Lorshe, commenting on this kind of dilemma says, "The issues involved are so complex that many managers oscillate between these two choices or try to effect some compromise between them."[6]

Expression/Survival

Peter Drucker said, "Organizations do not exist for their own sake, they are a means; each is society's organ for the discharge of one social task. Survival is not an adequate goal for an organization as it is for a biological species. The organization's goal is a specific contribution to individuals and to society. The test of its performance, unlike that of a biological organism, therefore always lies outside of it."[7] For Kenneth Galbraith the primary goal of an organization is to survive: "For any organization, as for any organism, the goal objective that has a natural assumption of pre-eminence is the organization's own survival."[8] One may well ask who is right.

Both are right: Galbraith perceives the organization as structure. He coined the word "techno-structure" and, what is significant to note, he did not coin the word "techno-process." Drucker perceives the organization as process. He developed the theory of management by objectives, which is essentially a process-oriented type of management.

Two contradictory tendencies are at work: an integrating or survival tendency and an expressive or mission tendency. The conflict between Drucker and Galbraith can be shown to be an example of one of the dilemmas facing management.

Summary

I want to show that work is a creative process, not a mechanical activity and that creativity arises in the face of incompatibility, or conflict. Work is the exercise of discretion within limits and these limits are, ultimately, incompatible. Another way of looking at these incompatible limits is to see them as dilemmas. I could then widen the definition to say that work is the exercise of discretion within the limits imposed by dilemmas. I have given samples of the kinds of dilemmas that managers are faced with, although many more could be found. Because employees have to deal with dilemmas as well as problems, work has two aspects: managerial and technical. As one ascends the management hierarchy, one encounters dilemmas more frequently, and the dilemmas are more complex than those of lower levels.

Let us go on now and explore in more detail the role of dilemmas in work.

Notes

1   Harry Levinson, *The Exceptional Executive* (Cambridge, MA: Harvard University Press, 1968), p. 34. "When a man works he has a contributing place in society. He earns the right to be the partner of other men. The fact that someone will pay for his work is an indication that others need what he does, and therefore that he is a necessary part of the social fabric. He matters as a man. To have a skill, trade, or occupation is to be a `who' and `what.'"
2   Irving Stone (ed.), *Dear Theo: Autobiography of Vincent van Gogh* (New York, Signet, 1937), p. 380.
3   Elliott Jaques, *Equitable Payment* (London: Heinemann, 1961), p. 71.
4   Peter Drucker, *The Age of Discontinuity* (New York: Harper and Row, 1969), p. 189.
5   A. H. Walker and J. W. Lorsche, "Organizational Choice: Product vs. Function," *Harvard Business Review*, Nov.–Dec. 1968, p. 130.
6   *Ibid.*, p. 131.
7   Drucker, *The Age of Discontinuity*, p. 87.
8   J. K. Galbraith, *The New Industrial State* (Boston: Houghton and Mifflin, 1971), p. 84.

CHAPTER SEVEN

The Dilemma at Work

To perform *managerial* work an employee must face and resolve dilemmas. If no dilemmas arose, managerial work would not be necessary. In this chapter I shall try to clarify further the dilemma underlying work and explain why it should in a way be called a *quadrilemma*, that is to say the situation has *four* conflicting horns, and not just the two horns of a dilemma. The quadrilemma shows the full structure of what is involved in work. I shall start by giving an example of a quadrilemma in a job in a gas utility.

The job of customer service representative

The job of customer service representative is to answer and deal with telephone calls from customers asking for service. The representative receives calls from customers, determines what they want, and completes a form. The first represents the managerial part of the job, the second — completing the form — is the technical part. The form will tell a serviceman to visit a customer's home to attend to the request by servicing the appliance or gas system. When the customer phones in, the call is put into a queue of calls from other customers. A recording explains that the line is busy for the time being and asks the customer to wait for a short while.

During most of the year, but particularly during the fall and early winter when furnaces must be cleaned and lit, many customers call at the same time, and the representative must work as quickly as possible to *get the customer off the line* so that others do not have to wait too long before receiving attention. On the other hand, the representative must *keep the customer on the line* to get accurate and relevant information, and to ensure that a service call is necessary. Customers sometimes call unnecessarily — some calls even come from people who do not own a gas appliance. Others have forgotten to switch their appliance on, or appliances do not work because the electrical equipment or fuses have failed. The customer can solve many problems himself provided sufficient

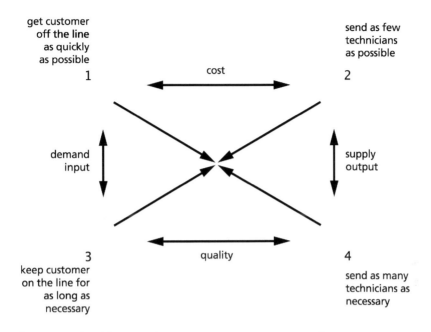

Figure 7.1 The dilemma of a customer service representative

instructions are given about what to do. This saves the company the cost of sending the technical representative to visit the customer.

A representative must balance these two incompatible alternatives: *get the customer off the line; keep the customer on the line*. But that is not all. The cost of sending a technical representative to a house to provide service is high. The representative is instructed to send out as few technical representatives as possible, and not to assign unnecessarily a high priority to a call. The more service calls and the higher the priority, the greater the cost. On the other hand, a utility must serve customers, and to ensure satisfaction a representative will sometimes have to send out a technical representative even though it may not be technically necessary to do so. For example, when roads are being asphalted customers frequently mistake the smell of asphalt for the smell of gas and phone the utility to complain of a gas leak. A representative getting a number of calls from the same location will identify the cause and explain this to the customers. Most will accept the explanation, but one or two will insist upon a service call being made.

Therefore a representative has two additional incompatible alternatives to balance: *send out technical representative, do not send out technical representative*, and these alternatives are related to the first two.

At corner number 1 is the statement, 'Get the customer off the line as quickly as possible in order to free the line'. That is the first requirement.

At corner number 3 is the statement, 'Keep the customer on the line as long as necessary to get sufficient information'. That is the second requirement and is incompatible with number 1.

At corner number 2 is the statement, 'Send out as few technical representatives as possible to keep costs low'. That is the third requirement. It is incompatible with number 1 but compatible with number 2.

At corner number 4 is the statement, 'Send out as many technical representatives as necessary to avoid customer dissatisfaction'. Statements 3 and 4 are incompatible. Statement 3 is compatible with statement 1, but incompatible with statement 4.

I said earlier that the basic limits of work were the cost/quality limits. I explained that these form the basic ambiguity. Corners 1 and 3 are both concerned with costs. The quicker the customer can be dealt with, the fewer representatives are necessary; the fewer technical representatives sent out, the fewer technical representatives have to be employed. Corners 2 and 4 are concerned with quality: listening carefully to the customer's problem and responding appropriately. These two criteria — cost and quality — form the basic limits of discretion that the representative uses to get results and to do work.

Corners 1 and 4, on the other hand, are complementary and so are comers 2 and 3. By keeping the customer on the line for as long as is required to investigate the call, the number of technical representatives being sent out to answer calls is reduced. The representative could give each customer a short course in appliance servicing and so eliminate almost all calls. But diminishing returns set in, and only so much can be said and done over the telephone. By simply asking each customer for his name and address and nothing else and then completing the order for a service call to be made, the representative could get each customer off the line with dispatch. But, of course, such a solution would be as unworkable as the short course on appliance servicing.

I have given a complete picture of the tensions at work within the customer inquiry system from the time the representative says, "Good morning, can I help you?" to when she says, "Thank you very much, good day," and goes on to the next customer. In other words, a continuous cycle goes on: tension, no tension, tension, no tension; or dilemma, absence of dilemma, dilemma, absence of dilemma.

The dilemma of salary administration

Let us now take another example of a dilemma: an administrative system dilemma. The same tensions are at work here:

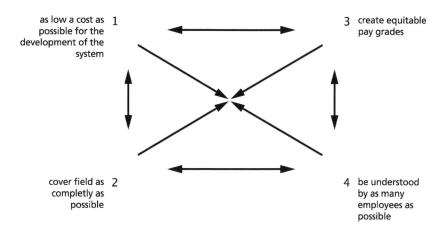

Figure 7.2 The dilemma of salary administration

A salary administration system is but one of a number of systems that the company needs. The salary administrator must therefore devise a system that will cost as little as possible in terms of resources and management time for setting it up and for operating it. The simpler and more streamlined, the better.

On the other hand, the system must be as complete as possible; all relevant jobs as well as all relevant elements of the jobs must be included. For example, if the system is designed for clerical employees, to leave out some clerical jobs or some elelements of jobs simply because of the difficulty or cost of including them in the study would be unwise. All relevant facts must be collected about all the jobs that are to be part of the system.

A conflict exists between these two considerations: a simple system and a complete system — the same conflict encountered in the earlier example. The more complete the system, the higher the cost is likely to be. The simpler the system, the more it becomes likely that something will be left out.

In addition, the system must be designed so that the employees whose salaries are governed by it are satisfied with it. They want their salaries to be administered equitably, and they want to be able to understand the system. These two requirements can be in conflict. An equitable salary system rewards different levels of work by corresponding levels of pay. With complete equity each job is given its correct level in a pay hierarchy. Ideally, a different pay grade should be created for each job. But to explain to an employee why his pay grade is at one level and a colleague's at a slightly higher level when the difference between the two jobs is barely perceptible would be a difficult problem. Borderline jobs bring with them this kind of problem. Borderline cases will always arise whenever we try to divide a continuum into segments, and the more pay grades, the more borderline cases.

Equality is easier to talk about than equity — people understand the word better than the word equity. Whereas with a completely equitable system each job has its own specific pay grade, with a completely equal system only one single grade would exist, with no borderline cases at all. Equity is based on the level of work that a person does; equality is based upon the needs that people have. The socialist ideal: 'from each according to his ability; to each according to his need', shows what I mean. Unions have a tendency to want to erode pay differentials as they find talking about equality to the rank and file is easier than talking about equity.

During a wage freeze imposed by the Canadian Government in the early seventies, a maximum dollar amount increase was imposed on companies. However, pay grades in most companies are based upon percentage differentials. Someone earning $50, 000 per year getting a 5 percent increase would receive $2,500; someone earning $100,000 per year getting the same percentage increase would receive $5,000. If the increases were restricted to $2,500, the first would still receive a 5 percent increase, but the second would receive a 2.5 percent increase. If they received $2,500, equality would be served, but not equity. Dollar and cent increases tend toward equality; percentage increases tend toward equity. Again a conflict arises.

Thus, in the illustration of a salary administration system (Figure 7.2), corners 1 and 2 are in opposition and so are corners 3 and 4, while corners 1 and 4 are complementary. The less complex the system is, the easier it is to communicate. In fact, people often say, "Let's keep it simple," meaning "Let's make it easy to communicate." Corners 2 and 3 are complementary. The more complete and thorough, the greater the chance of equity being reached.

Furthermore, two internal aspects are concerned with the system and two external aspects are concerned with acceptance of the system: the first two concern the makeup of the system, the second two, the reception that others give it.

The basic dilemma

If all managerial work is concerned with the resolution of dilemmas, can the insights gained from the study of the job of the customer service representative and the job of setting up a salary administration system be

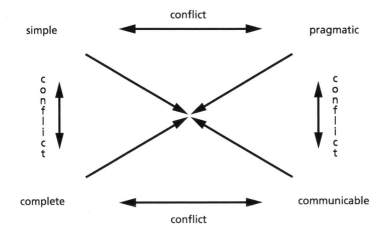

Figure 7.3 The basic dilemma

extended to become a general principle related to all jobs? If so, we could establish a paradigm that could be used to identify the particular dilemma underlying any particular job. The dilemma would thus be brought into consciousness and so made easier to be dealt with. At present a manager must often deal with dilemmas at a preconscious, and therefore inarticulate, level. The actions he takes may be correct, but because they are inarticulate and intuitive they cannot always be adequately explained, nor are they always as simple as they could be if they were exposed to the light of conscious reason.

Four criteria can be used to judge a theory, organization, or system: simplicity, completeness, and pragmatism (does the job do what it is supposed to do?)[1] and communicability. They are related as in Figure 7.3.

The importance of the dilemma

The dilemma, or its intellectual counterpart the paradox, is, as C. G. Jung points out, essential if one is to describe a complete system. "Oddly enough, the paradox is one of our most valuable spiritual possessions, while uniformity of meaning is a sign of weakness . . . only the paradox comes anywhere near to comprehending the fullness of life. Non-ambiguity and non-contradiction are one-sided and thus unsuited to express the incomprehensible."[2] Our understanding of a company is impoverished when we ignore or reject ambiguity and dilemmas.

The dilemma not only underlies work, but all human activity. Talking about the dilemma or ambiguity is complicated and what is said is often difficult to understand. But because they lead us to the core of work itself — to its difficulty — and even to the very core of life, dilemma and ambiguity cannot be neglected. Again quoting Jung: "Scientific integrity forbids all simplification of situations that are not simple."[3]

Another look at stress

The question: "What makes work difficult?" has recurred frequently. We have come to the conclusion that much of the difficulty comes from the stress generated by dilemmas. Nevertheless, many who have written on management theory have pointed out that people enjoy work, and that failure to find work that is sufficiently challenging causes the personality to deteriorate. These two statements — that work generates tension and that work is desirable — seem to be contradictory, because people obviously seem to want to get rid of tension and stress. The mind could even be considered to be a tension-reduction system.

If, however, the mind is seen only as a tension-reduction system, we should find forms of behavior that are impossible to understand. For example, why do people go to see horror movies; in fact, why do people go to see any film or play at all? A good drama goes through a steady build-up of tension; Shakespeare, for example, would build up tension and then, by employing humor, release some of it, only so that more tension could be built up subsequently. Why do people climb mountains, race cars, ski, or gamble?

Two tendencies appear to be at work in us, and the mind appears to be a tension-induction/reduction system. Each of us has a certain tension, or stress, tolerance, and our aim is to match the tolerance of tension to the work at hand. If the tension is too high we seek to reduce the level of work to the level of tolerance; on the other hand, if it is too low we seek to increase the level of work and so increase the level of tension.

Sometimes we feel under-worked, and so look around for more to do. We continue to do so until we feel overworked, and then we try to let go of work until the feeling of being under-worked returns. Observing oneself over a period of several months, one might find that one goes through a fairly regular cycle of overwork/under-work. Parkinson's law expressed half of the cycle — work expands to fill the vacuum created by more time — while the Peter Principle — people are promoted to their level of incompetence — expresses the other half.

We seem to need tension, but tension under control. As long as tension is under control, life is interesting. When tension exceeds the point of tolerance life becomes unbearable. Many people leave one job for another because they feel that the earlier job offers too little challenge, and challenge is what creates tension in them. Most of us find boredom to be one of the worst experiences, and boredom arises when a plateau has been reached and the situation no longer generates enough tension.

The work situation is therefore a creation that has great psychological value. Through work we can escape the effects of the basic contradiction in our being by projecting it as the dilemmas of the work situation. When working in a well-organized company our wound, the basic schism, is, as it were, caged, and we are able to enjoy its power without seemingly paying its price. Work is not the invention of Western society; its contribution has been to deify work. Industrial employment work is modern society's answer to a religionless society. Religion, in past societies, provided the source of the work for human beings, and through spiritual work, also known as the Great Work, religion showed them how to go beyond the dilemma. The mandala of the Buddhists and the cross of the Christians are symbols of the conflicting forces to which we are subject, and of the degree of suffering that these forces can create.

Notes

1   These four criteria can also be used to assess the value of a theory. Some theories have value because they bring together a great deal of otherwise unrelated information. Darwin's theory of evolution is an example. This kind of theory has heuristic rather than practical value.

2   C. G. Jung, tr. R. F. C. Hull, *Psychology and Religion West and East* (London: Routledge & Kegan Paul, 1953), p. 15.

3   *Ibid.*, p. 221.

CHAPTER EIGHT

Management by Product

Work is the exercise of discretion within limits in order to produce a result. I have written at length about the limits that call for the exercise of discretion, and have shown that they take the form of dilemmas that often require a creative resolution. Now the meaning of the word *result* must be clarified. Quite obviously the result cannot be just any result but must have value to the company as a whole. Let us say that the result produced is a *product*. This chapter will be devoted to exploring what the word *product* means.

A product is an idea in a form with a demand

When talking about organization to groups of managers in the company for which I worked, I would pose the question, "What is a product?" Even though a product is central to the life of a company, managers were hard pressed to come up with a decent answer. And managers are not alone in having this difficulty. Looking up the word in the dictionary *Encarta* I find that it says that a product is, "something that is made or created by a person, machine, or natural process, especially something that is offered for sale", or "something that arises as a consequence of something else". Neither of these is very helpful.

To bring home in a concrete way the meaning of the word 'product' I would hold up a fairly small, roughly cut, wedge-shaped piece of wood, and ask, "Is this a product?" Most of those present would say no, saying further that the piece of wood was useless and no one would want to buy it. When they were pressed though, someone would likely seize on its shape and suggest that it could be used as a doorstop. He or she would say, "Someone could use it to keep a door open." I would then pull from my pocket and show them a rubber doorstop that is sold in the local hardware store. The rubber doorstop is only slightly more elegant than the wedge of wood, yet everyone agreed that it was a product. I would then ask what was the magic that transformed the useless wedge of wood into a product? Most of the managers would immediately recognize that the piece of wood became a product when someone had an *idea*.

A product is an idea in a form. In the case of the doorstop, the material of which the *form* is made is not very important: it can be made of wood, metal, rubber, or plastic. Nevertheless, the *idea* is constant: a wedge-shaped something that can be pushed under a door. But the definition of a product as an idea in a form is not complete. Only when the block-of-wood-that-could-be-a-doorstop is put into juxtaposition with doors that one wants to keep open — in other words, when a demand is envisaged — does the block of wood truly take on the characteristics of a product. *A product is therefore an idea in a form with a demand.*

An idea

The definition that I gave of creativity included the word 'idea': a single idea in two incompatible frames of reference. Just as an idea transformed the block of wood into a doorstop, so, when you were working on the illustration of the hidden man, the idea transformed the mess of black and white shapes into a face. What then is an idea?

Most of us believe that everything in principle is knowable. Scientists work with this belief. If someone talks about something that is unknowable, we believe he or she has wandered into some New Age never-never land. Even so an idea is unknowable because we need that idea to know that idea. In a similar way we cannot see the eye because, to be able to see, we need the eye. How can you talk about that which you need to have in order to be able talk about it? Anything that can be said about the idea is not the idea, but an expression of an idea about the idea.[1]

Perhaps I should say what the word 'idea', in the way that I am using it, does not mean. It is *not* a thought, although it may be expressed by a thought; when I think *about* an idea I am thinking thoughts, although these, if I am thinking intelligently, are guided by an idea. But an idea can be expressed through music, painting, dancing, gestures, or symbols. Idea is not to be found separate from experience. In other words, 'it' (idea) is not a 'spiritual' or 'mystical' thing that floats in some unworldly, Platonic ether. Neither is it the opposite of reality, the opposite of something more substantial like a rock, a brick, or a pile of gold, as expressed by "Oh! That's just an idea; it's not real." Idea is not 'something', it is not single or general, and the words 'it', 'an' idea, or 'the' idea are used only because language demands we designate it somehow. Even though I cannot really talk about it, nevertheless all intelligent talk is the expression of an idea. An idea is not, then, nothing. The very coherence of the world as we see it depends upon the world-idea, (or *weltanschauung*), that we have of it. Moreover as you try to understand what I am now saying you seek an idea that will contain it in a meaningful way, just as you sought an idea to contain the black and white shapes in a meaningful way.

The notion of idea is, of course, very important philosophically, and many philosophers have struggled to say what the word means. The notion is, nonetheless, of practical importance in the world of commerce and industry. The level of a product, and therefore of a company, is a function of the level of the idea of which that product is the expression. Furthermore, the potential for growth that a company has is directly related to the level of the primary product of that company, that is the primary idea in a form with a demand. The railroads stopped growing even though the need for transportation increased. The decline of railways did not occur because the need was filled by others, but simply because it was not filled by the railroads themselves. The railroads allowed others to take customers away from them because they assumed themselves to be in the railroad business rather than in the transportation business. The reason they defined their industry wrongly was because the *idea* they had was railroad-oriented instead of transportation-oriented.[2] Hollywood also had the wrong idea about its business and suffered as a consequence. "It thought it was in the movie business when it was really in the entertainment business. 'Movies' implies a specific limited product"[3] (i.e., lower level idea).

Cecil Rhodes, the British explorer, told queen Victoria that his ambition was to build a railroad from Cape Town to Cairo. The queen is reputed to have said, "But Cecil, *you*, in the railroad business!?" Rhodes replied, "No ma'am, in the Empire building business."

Peter Drucker underlines the importance of the company idea when he asks, "Is a company that makes and sells kitchen appliances, such as electric ranges, in the food business? Is it in the homemaking business? Or is it's main business really consumer finance? Each answer might be the right one at a given time for a given company. But each would lead to very different conclusions as to where the company should put its efforts and seek its rewards."[4] The answer depends upon the idea.

Let me quote a philosopher, Jacques Maritain, who speaks about this 'idea' in his book *Intuition in Poetry and the Arts*. The Schoolmen were the philosophers of the Middle Ages.

> This determinative focus is what the Schoolmen called the *idea factiva* that is to say the 'creative idea.' They took care, moreover, to warn us that the craftsman's creative idea is in no way a concept, for it is neither cognitive nor representative, it is only generative; it does not tend to make our mind conform to things, but to make a thing conform to our mind. They never

even used the word 'idea' in the sense of 'concept' as we have done since the time of Descartes.[5]

Although one may not be able to say what an idea is, one can say what it does. The word 'idea' has its etymological roots in a Greek word *idein*, which means 'to see'. *An idea reveals relations between phenomena*. Let me refer to the exercise on perception. What enabled you to see those black and white shapes as a face? It was an idea. The idea showed you how the shapes could be related to each other in the simplest and most complete way, a way in which you used as many of the black and white shapes as possible.

Moreover, when we perceive elements in relation as a system rather than as separate units, we perceive a new unity. If you are reading this book at home and you look around you will see a room, you do not see a collection of pieces of furniture plus four walls, a ceiling and a floor. An idea enables you to see the room as a whole.. Whereas in the absence of an idea you see unrelated shapes, in the presence of an idea each element has its relation to all other elements. The idea gives meaning to what was otherwise meaninglessness. Through the idea perception is guided by a tendency to perceive units or 'ones'. The categorical imperative, "Let there be one!" guides our perception and therefore one could say that *idea is the eye of unity*.

A *fact* on the other hand expresses those relations that an idea reveals. It comes into being by expressing the idea. We are inclined to believe that a fact is a mental construct only, yet we would do well to remember that the word 'fact' is derived from the Latin *facere*, which means 'to do' or 'to make'. From *facere* is also derived the French word *fait*, which means 'do', 'make', and 'fact'. What a person makes or does derives from the idea that he or she has. All human artifacts are in a way 'facts'. People originally manu*fac*tured, that is to say they used their hands to express the idea as a fact or form. (In Latin, *manus* means 'hand'). With the rise of capitalism, machines have taken the place of hands, but manufacturing is still basically the expression of an idea through a form even though it may occur in factories.

The form of a product corresponds to the relations revealed by an idea. In other words, form fixes the relations. Ideas alone are in demand; old-time salesmen knew that they should 'sell the sizzle and not the steak'; they knew they had to sell the idea, not just the form the idea took.

But, a product is not simply an idea in a form. A demand for the idea must exist before a product is produced, and the market provides the demand. A form frames the evanescence of an idea, but it is demand that makes it real. By demand I mean *need, with the willingness and ability to work, which means to pay, to have the need satisfied.* Through demand the form meshes or fits in with other forms. Through demand a link or interchange is established between the company-as-product and its environment.

A world of ideas

Wherever you look you will see ideas that have been put into forms that have a demand: a pen, a desk, a room, or a building, were originally someone's idea. Some of these ideas subsume a great number of other ideas. A car, for instance, subsumes thousands of ideas, including those that are subsumed by the engine, the car body, the transmission, and the wheels, as well as those that are subsumed in traffic laws, maps, and roads. Henry Ford was one of the first to have the idea of the automobile; an architect conceived the building you are in; Bell first perceived the idea of a telephone, and Edison the idea of an electric light bulb; the Earl of Sandwich first had the idea of a sandwich. Whether or not the author is known, the idea originated with a human being. Some ideas can be specifically traced to their origin, others cannot. Who first perceived the idea of a wheel? Who perceived the idea of a tie as being suitable apparel for men?

Form enables an idea to become 'something'. Human beings fix their ideas in matter and so express their ideas. The expression imposes limits upon the idea, isolates it, separates it from all others, and so makes it 'a thing'.

It becomes difficult to find the boundaries of an object when it is looked at as a set of ideas. An automobile melts into subsumed and subsuming and interacting ideas of steel, rubber, gasoline; ideas of friction and compression; ideas of fleets of cars, tanks, and jeeps; ideas of vacations, business trips, and visits to friends. An automobile is a system of ideas — ideas that stand in mutual relation with each other while each retains its integrity and independence. Ideas reveal relations between phenomena expressed in form in a beginingless and endless flux.

A very useful exercise would be to visit a museum and see a model of the old log cabins. See how few ideas are expressed in it. Then wander around your own home and see how many ideas are expressed in it. But do not start with the computer for you will never get beyond it. It is nested within ideas nested within ideas. If you look around you then you will realize that what you perceive you only perceive through the idea, and you will see that it is truer to say that we live *in a world of ideas*[6] than that we live in a physical world.

The power of idea

If you paint the kitchen, or cook a meal, or rearrange the furniture you are giving expression to an idea. What is more, when you have an idea you have the energy to give it form, but when you lose the idea you can no longer be bothered. For example, have you noticed that when you paint the kitchen you want to keep going until you have finished? It may be getting very late, you may be feeling quite tired, but, even so you keep going until the job is done. Then, next day, you see a small patch at the bottom of a wall that you missed that still needs painting. You just do not have the energy to do it. Weeks, months, even years may pass and that patch of unpainted wall remains. The idea has gone. The presence of an idea focuses commitment and so generates the energy necessary to accomplish work. As the old adage would have it: nothing is so powerful as an idea whose time has come; perhaps one can add that nothing is so weak as an idea whose time has passed.

The form of a product is not always material

In the manufacturing process the material so often provides the form but this is only incidental. Modern industry is seeing a rapid increase in work directed simply to expressing ideas in verbal form. That we live in the age of information is a common belief, but to say we live in an age of ideas would be nearer the truth. The distinction is important because although computers may process information, only human beings 'process' ideas; no machine will ever process ideas.

Much of the work performed at middle and senior management level, much management consulting work, is simply the expression of ideas in a verbal form through reports, financial statements, contracts, systems and decisions. The result of work done by a financial, engineering, or industrial relations consultant is just as much a product as the result of a heavy steel worker or an automobile engineer. A medical diagnosis is a product, and so is a lecture. A lecture may be written or given orally, it may be fixed in laboratory apparatus, or given incidentally to the process of constructing, maintaining, or operating a machine. In any case, it is a product as I have defined the word.

The use of material, such as plastic, steel, or rubber is just one way to make an idea endure; ideas are also captured by the mind through language. A word is an idea in a form. Words are products, and just as one product subsumes another product, so some words or elements of language subsume others.

Normally the economist does not consider banking to be a product.

He considers it to be a service. But a service is still an idea in a form with a demand. The idea is readily accessible finances, and the form is ATM, the bankcard, the check, the bank statement, the overdraft, etc. I use the word 'product' to refer to any idea in a form with a demand and will include those services provided by a bank, insurance company, or a hotel.

Putting the total human being backing the picture

The recognition of the product as an idea in a form with a demand, and therefore of the idea being the central and dominating value in a company, puts the total human being back into the industrial scene. The perception and realization of an idea is the work of employees.[7] "A business devoted to the identification of central ideas, the formulation of strategies for moving swiftly from ideas to operations, will differ in structure and activity from a company primarily concerned with management of money or physical resources."[8]

Once upon a time the major concern in industry was materials handling. The organization of many companies was, to a large degree, devoted to ensuring that people did not get in the way of the material. But to survive in the future the problem for industry will be increasingly one of idea generation. The rapidity with which the market can change is arguably the greatest challenge that companies face at the moment. As long as attention is given primarily to the form of the product, the necessary flexibility to respond to the change will be absent. A company could be looked upon as an organism whose primary food is ideas. Ideas originate from employees. They conceive the idea and find ways to give it form. But they can only do so if they are *committed*. Without the commitment, as was shown in the example of painting the kitchen, they will not have the energy to generate the idea or be able to sustain the energy long enough for the idea to be given form.

On management by product

Management by product is a broader yet more concrete concept than management by objectives, or strategic planning. In some of the more advanced industries, top management has defined a core idea around which the total company effort can be designed, such as "a shift in the definition of a business from one concerned with the sale of a product to one concerned with the delivery of a complete system of customer values — as in airlines marketing packaged vacations and computer manufacturers marketing systems to solve customers' information problems."[9] The major product of some companies is the brand name, which incorporates a whole range of products and even points to a life style. "Ideas are the energized core of a unique design for a business. The exploitation of each idea requires a comprehensive intellectual grasp of the totality of a business viewed as an interacting system."[10] The task demands, "special intellectual ability to visualize the translation of *ideas and strategies* into controlled operating systems responsive to dynamic change"[11] (emphasis added).

Notes

1 'Me' is the very first idea that we have of ourselves. A child, at about the age of two, for the first time begins to know himself or herself as a separate person, 'me'. Normally we say that the child becomes 'self-conscious', or 'self-aware'. The child reflects on itself or, to be more precise, awareness is turned back on itself, and the idea 'me', by containing the dilemma that this creates, resolves it.

2 Theodore Levitt, "Marketing Myopia," *Harvard Business Review*, July–August 1960, pp. 275–76.

3 *Ibid.*, p. 276.

4 Drucker, *The Age of Discontinuity*, p. 190.

5 Jacques Maritain, *Creative Intuition in Art and Poetry* (New York: Meridian Books, 1955), p. 100.

6 The philosopher, Karl Popper, conceived of a 'Third World', a world of ideas in which we live. The other two worlds are the physical world of things and the subjective world of feelings, thoughts and sensation.

7 Melvin Anshen, "The Management of Ideas," *Harvard Business Review*, July–August 1969, pp. 99–107.

8 *Ibid.*, p. 102.

9 *Ibid.*, p. 101.

10 *Ibid.*, p. 101.

11 *Ibid.*, p. 102.

CHAPTER NINE

Idea and the Four Criteria

The notion of 'idea' is very important. The definition that I have been using for creativity is 'an idea in two mutually exclusive frames of reference'. Furthermore, the outcome of work is a product that is an *idea* in a form with a demand. By producing a product the many conflicting tendencies of a company are resolved creatively, which enables the company to be self-regulating and able to grow. Let us explore further why in the West we have difficulty understanding what the word 'idea' means.

André Lamouche, the chief architect of the French Navy, said, "It is more difficult to make truth known than it is to discover truth. Furthermore, as the propositions one is making become more general, the complications involved in bringing out the meaning increase and so do the difficulties in being precise."[1] When I talk about 'the basic schism or wound', 'the dilemma', and 'the idea', I am talking about the most general of notions; they are not abstract and philosophical but, on the contrary, they underlie our entire experience and make it possible and real. Yet, just as one sees with the eye but the eye cannot see itself, so although 'the wound', 'the dilemma', and 'the idea', make experience possible, *they themselves cannot be experienced*. But one cannot conclude that they are not real.

In spite of the difficulty of communication, because 'idea' is so important to understanding human behavior at work and elsewhere, I would like, in as practical a way as possible, to make its meaning as clear as possible. If I can do so then I can talk more meaningfully about the problems of work and organization.

The lack of understanding of the importance of idea

Although the notion of 'idea' is important, little mention is made of it in management literature. In the modern Western world we are severely hampered in gaining an understanding of what it means principally because of the dominance of the rationalistic, positivistic approach based on classical logic. This is particularly true in America where behaviorism and materialism, both of which set narrow and artificial limitations upon what is acceptable as knowledge, have flourished for so long. And so, ideas, consciousness, and intention, when they are not looked upon as verbal fictions, are thought to be just bye-products of the interaction of matter. They are thought to have no meaning of their own, and, moreover, the idea is thought to have no creative function.

Without the notion of the creative idea we cannot even broach the subject of creativity or work, as literature of behaviorism shows. How, for example, does the behaviorist believe that a new creation comes into being, such as a poem, an essay, a management report, or a new practice or procedure in a company, or even a new company product? J. B. Watson, an early behaviorist, asks, " How do you suppose that Patou builds a new gown? Has he any picture in his mind of what the gown is to look like when it is finished? He has not . . . He calls his model in, picks up a piece of silk, throws it around her, he pulls it in here and pulls it out there . . . He manipulates the material until it takes on the semblance of a dress. . . . Not until the creation aroused admiration and commendation, both his own and others, would manipulation be completed — the equivalent of a rat's finding food . . . The painter plies his trade in the same way, nor can the poet boast of any other,"[2] nor, presumably, can the manager. According to Watson, NASA presumably took some metal, punched it here and bored it there, and not until it was universally admired was it sent to the moon as a rocket.

One thing that the behaviorists say that I can agree with is that Patou, NASA or any manager are not likely to have a picture or image in his mind when they work. Instead they have an idea, an idea that guides them to their destination, to their product. The idea is then put in contest with other ideas and with the environment to learn whether it is fit enough to survive.

The field of the hidden man is best structured by the idea of a man, or rather the idea of the head and torso of a man. This idea can structure the field with such clarity a discussion can take place between two people about the field. The picture is that of a bearded man, but to say this to someone who has not perceived the face in the field simply creates confusion and blankness. At work we are also faced with situations having conflicting ambiguities and dilemmas and are called upon to bring order into them. We too are called upon to create a 'best structure' for these situations, although we may not structure them quite as precisely as we structure the black and white field.

Four criteria

By the expression 'best structure' I mean that the structure is in accord with the *four criteria* discussed in chapter seven. The structure must be as *complete* as possible — that is, one must use as much of the field as possible — but the structure also must be as *simple* as possible. It must be structured *meaningfully*: the words 'practical' or 'heuristic' could be used equally well. Finally it must be structured in a way that others can agree that it is structured in the best way so that it will find its place in a wider environment. This is the *communication* criterion.

When you worked to see the face, the idea that you finally created had to meet these four criteria. By doing the work the black-and-white confusion was changed into a face. Our commitment to find order in chaos, to structure what is otherwise unstructured, to find a pattern, brings the idea to birth. The idea was not present in the black and white shapes. Had it been present then no work would have been necessary, and everyone would readily perceive the face without the necessity for the work. The idea, then, is a new creation even though others may have had it before you did.

As you might remember, an important fact emerged from the exercise: the face did not appear in stages. It appeared complete, whole, or it did not appear at all. The drive to find order in a chaotic situation, out of which the idea emerges, comes from the drive to unity. Hence, I have said that the idea is *the eye of unity*.

The hidden man and everyday life

The field in figure 2.1 (page 27), the hidden man, is similar to the field of phenomena that we encounter in everyday life. Our surroundings are in a state of confusion until we are able to structure them through an idea. The film, *What the Bleep do we know?* tells us that the Mayans could not see the Spanish ships when they first arrived. Eventually the shaman saw the ships, and he told others about them. Because these had faith in him, they looked in the direction where the ships were supposed to be, and, after looking for a while, they finally saw them. When you go to a company as a new employee, for some time the place seems a total confusion. Gradually you manage to sort out the geography and so find your way around more easily.

Another example of these confusions and tensions is given when you are driving along the highway and come to some kind of confusion in the road. If you happen to be driving in a snowstorm or through thick mist and fog, the work involved in structuring can be quite exhausting.

Everyday life has many more dimensions than the two shown in the illustration of the hidden man, and it is of course much more complex. Nevertheless, we are constantly called upon to structure the field of everyday life in such a way as to overcome the confusions and tensions brought about by lack of order.

Figure 9.1 Patterns

Not only is the field often a complex one and hard to organize, but, as the example of the young/old woman showed, it can be organized in ambiguous ways. Much of the conflict that arises in industry arises out of ambiguity. Because many managers may be involved, the field can be structured, not only in two, but in many different ways, and each of them could be quite legitimate. A particular manager, by the way his job is set up, is expected to perceive only one of these ways. Indeed, he is paid, promoted, and his self-esteem is reinforced to the extent that he is able to exploit that particular way, so conflict is endemic within a company.

Patterns

Figure 9.1 illustrates another aspect of 'idea'. At first glance one sees the field as a chaotic black-and-white field with little regularity. Normally most people then see the wind-mill-shaped patterns dispersed about the field. If, though, you study the field further you will see other patterns begin to emerge, and the longer you study it the more intricate the patterns become. Because of dynamic unity our minds do not simply accept a chaotic field, they try instead to structure the field and so make it simpler while retaining as much of the field as possible.

Figure 9.1 shows that, by increasing the level of idea we are able to make increasingly complex patterns. These, in turn make it possible to take in more of the field and the structure is correspondingly more complete. If you pay close attention to what you are doing when you look at the figure, you will see that that your mind builds up patterns, and when as much as possible of the field has been included within that pattern, it releases the idea, allows the field to return to its original state of chaos, then builds up new patterns, with a new idea, in the hope of integrating even more phenomena within a single grasp. As the pattern becomes more complex, the structure becomes increasingly unstable, and has a greater tendency toward disintegration.

Towards simplicity and completeness

The hidden man, the old and young woman and figure 9.1 showed the tendency of the mind to preserve as much as possible of the field — that is, to be complete — but at the same time to remain one, simple. Figure 9.1 illustrates the dilemma: to maintain a simple pattern some of the field had to be rejected; but one wants to include the entire field. As one went in the direction of completion the simple patterns started to disintegrate. The same thing occurs with scientific research. The scientist comes up with a theory that simplifies the field. Other scientists point out that data

Figure 9.2 The three men

has been left out, the theory is abandoned and a new theory is created.

The next two illustrations give further evidence that through an idea the mind tends towards simplicity as well as completeness. But they also show the problems encountered by the mind when it attempts to do so.

One of the men in figure 9.2 seems to be much larger than the other two. Indeed many people have to measure the three men to convince themselves that the figures are in fact of the same size. The mind simplifies the field by integrating the converging lines with the figures by accepting the lines as perspective. Although the idea is simple and complete one rejects it because it does not conform to the third criterion, that is to say it is not practical.

The picture of three triangles illustrates yet another tendency, the tendency to simplify towards meaning, that is towards the third criterion as well as the fourth criterion, communication. First read the words in each triangle quite quickly. Do so several times and a striking fact will suddenly appear: A word is duplicated in each triangle! Most people will read what is in the triangle several times before the fact emerges. This simple demonstration shows the tendency of the mind to simplify as much as possible, to eliminate unnecessary elements in order to make

Figure 9. 3 Simplifying

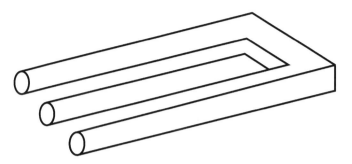

Figure 9.4 The Tuning Fork

the statements meaningful.

One final picture will show what we already know: the mind can run into difficulties when it attempts to both simplify and be complete. By looking at the picture from one end or the other, the figure is a simple whole. But the figure itself contains a contradiction. The picture presents a dilemma. The mind finds it as satisfactory to accept completeness as it does simplicity, and equally unsatisfactory to sacrifice either.

In attempting to describe the way people structure a field I have used the word 'mind', a word that is likely to cause some difficulties. 'Mind' is often thought of as a receptacle of experience — something like a cup that is filled, or a slate that is written upon. We can see from the above that the 'mind' is intensely active and dynamic, seeking unity as completeness and at the same time unity as simplicity.

Summary

Let me sum up as succinctly as I can where we have got to so far. The impulse to live, to survive, act, work and create comes from what I have called dynamic unity. The impulse could be called will or intention, commitment or dedication, depending on the circumstances. Although the impulse is a drive to unity, nevertheless, within the original viewpoint, dynamic unity is turned back on itself. Consciously we know this as self-awareness, self-reflection or even self-consciousness. Yet upstream of the conscious mind unity turning back on itself creates an implacable dilemma. The various emotions, ways of thinking and perceiving are all conditioned by it.[4] The dilemma, therefore, is at the core of our being and comes from the basic schism, and it is central to understanding work and organization.

The two extremes represented by the horns of the dilemma create limits in which all actions in life are performed. These actions in turn come from attempts to restore lost harmony and unity. The four criteria: the simple, complete, pragmatic, and communicable, emerge from the drive to unity and condition the way we perceive, think, act, and, of course, work.

The most immediate way that dynamic unity shows itself is in perception (of an idea) and its expression as fact. I have put 'of an idea' in brackets because, as I have explained, perception must include perception of an idea. We cannot perceive phenomena that have not been structured by an idea. I have said that a product is an idea in a form with a demand, and now I have shown the kind of difficulties that we can have when dealing with an idea, which must be simple, complete, practical and able to be communicated.

Notes

1   André Lamouche, *Le Principe de Simplicité dans les Mathematiques et les Sciences Physiques* (Paris: La Colombe, 1963), p. 25.

2   J. B. Watson, *Behaviorism* (Chicago: University of Chicago Press, 1930), p. 198.

3   For more on this see Albert Low, *Creating Consciousness: A study of consciousness, creativity, evolution and violence* (Oregon: White Cloud Press, 2001).

4   See, Low, *Creating Consciousness* and Albert Low, *The Origin of Human Nature: A Zen Buddhist looks at evolution* (Brighton & Portland: Sussex Academic Press, 2008).

PART THREE

The Company Field

CHAPTER TEN

The Three Power-holders

Starting with the 'hidden man' experiment, the notion of a field, and the need to structure the field by an idea, have been constant themes throughout all that I have said so far. A work situation, a department, a company a conglomerate, these are all *fields*. The next few chapters will be devoted to exploring what I mean when I refer to these as fields.

The myth

In 1966 when I was researching material for the book *Zen and Creative Management*, I had the opportunity to talk with several different groups of management consultants. On one occasion I was giving a talk to some financial consultants who had been engaged by the company for which I was working. I was expressing my belief that a company was best looked at as a field of forces, and that we could not view a company simply as a machine by which return to the stockholder alone is maximized. This caused an immediate outburst of protests from the group. One member of the group lifted his chair, turned it around so its back was facing me, and then sat down, and he continued to sit like that, with his back firmly turned towards me, for the rest of the discussion.

It was a visceral rejection. I have encountered similar kinds of rejection and have often found it difficult to have a reasonable discussion on this question; so much so that I have come to the conclusion that the belief that a company is in business to make a profit is a very deep-seated myth. In order to be sure that I am right to use the word myth, I looked up its meaning, first in the *Encarta World English Dictionary* and then in *Webster's New Collegiate Dictionary*. According to the first, 'mythical' means "not true or real, but existing only in somebody's imagination." According to *Webster's Dictionary* myth "serves to unfold part of the world view of a people or to explain a practice, belief, or natural phenomena." Webster also says that a myth is "an ill-founded belief held uncritically." An on line encyclopedia said, "A myth may be broadly defined as a narrative that through many retellings has become an accepted tradition in a society."

Marjorie Kelly, in her book, *The Divine Right of Capital* says, "This myth found its most forceful articulation in the 1919 Michigan Supreme Court case of *Dodge v. Ford Motor Company*, which established that 'A business company is organized and carried on primarily for the profit of the stockholders.'"[1] She quotes Lawrence Mitchell, the George Washington University Law professor who wrote, "Dodge v Ford remains the leading case on corporate purpose."[2] Nobel Prize winning economist Milton Friedman endorses the court ruling, and says that the *only* social responsibility a company has is to make a profit.

The myth of profit for the shareholder has become accepted as a given truth in our society; it is backed by law and supported by academic authority. In spite of its being deeply entrenched in the psyche, the myth of such a univalent view of a company must be abandoned and replaced by a multivalent view if we are to have real knowledge about the corporate system. It will take time for this replacement to occur because the myth is deeply embedded. Even so, in the last thirty to forty years the power of the myth of the patriarchal society has been reduced substantially and so it should be possible to reduce the power of the myth that a company is in business *simply* to maximize the return on investment of the stockholder.

A triad of forces

This myth of a company is simple but not complete, as it does not agree with all the facts. Those who defend the profit motive rightly point out that if a company does not make a profit — that is, if it does not satisfy the needs of the stockholders — then they will withdraw their support and the company will decline. But, the employees and customers can also withdraw their support. Should one or other do so the results would be just as dire as the stockholders withdrawing theirs. A triad of forces is involved in the creation and maintenance of a company, not just a single force. The work of employees sustains a company and ideas generated by employees are the lifeblood of a company; so obviously, if the employees work for the sake of the stockholders, the stockholders must also invest for the sake of the employees.

Ironically, much of the criticism I received for saying that a company is not in business simply for the stockholders' benefit came from fellow managers. They assured me that business was no place for sentiment, and that I had to face the hard facts of life. Yet these same hardheaded realists were claiming that they were altruistically prepared to put the interests of unknown, anonymous and faceless stockholders ahead of their own!

The economist, Kenneth Galbraith believed that a company exists for the employees; that is, the techno-structure: "The association of men of diverse technical knowledge, experience, or other talent which modern industrial technology and planning require. It extends from the leadership of the modern enterprise down to just short of the labor force."[3] No doubt a sufficient number of union leaders would want to know why Galbraith stops "just short of the labor force." Galbraith does not believe the company is ethically obliged to serve the market or the stockholder. On the contrary, "so far from being controlled by the market, the firm to the best of its ability has made the market subordinate to the goals of it's planning."[4] Galbraith is equally categorical when he says that profit maximization is no longer necessary.

Management guru Peter Drucker has a different view. For him the primary task of a company is to produce a product and to fulfill a particular role in society. Drucker feels that the goal of serving society through the market is an ethical obligation. He also tends to dismiss or play down the importance of employees' needs and wants. "The large business organization does not exist for the sake of the employees. Its results lie outside and are only tangentially affected by employee approval, consent and attitude."[5]

Wilfred Brown[6] wrote quite extensively on management. He was the Chairman of the Glacier Metal Industry and wrote from considerable personal experience as a practicing manager. He said that three power groups controlled a company: stockholders, customers and employees. He said that referring to customers as a power group may seem far-fetched, but experience shows the justification of doing so. Customers can, in fact, close a company down by withdrawing their custom if they dislike its products, prices, or delivery dates,. He said that the employees also possess great power and can close the company down by going on strike. Thus a power group is a group that can, in principle, close down the company.

These forces, although quite different from each other, have equal status within a company. Not only do all three have equal powers — because each can close the company down — all three are equally investors. To talk of a 'company' having this or that attitude or obligation to stockholders, employees or the market is nothing more than a way of talking, because the company *is* its employees, its stockholders and its market. While the law may recognize a company as a person, clear perception, which the law rarely has, is that this 'person' is a multidimensional field of forces. That is why I refer to the stockholder, employee and market *dimension*. Even so, for the sake of simplicity and clarity, when appropriate I will continue to use the expression 'the company'.

A stockholder

A stockholder invests money because he has some available that he does not wish to have lying idly in a bank. In making an investment he will look for the greatest liquidity, the highest return and the lowest risk possible. He also wants to see the investment grow over the years, and will sometimes be prepared to receive a relatively low immediate return from the investment in the form of dividends, or have less liquidity, if he feels confident that this will be balanced by a fairly high and sustained growth. He can sell shares that he has invested in a particular company and invest it in another, but if he has a large investment he may well lose money in the process. He would also probably need to do a fair amount of research before making the move. This research can be quite a complex process and he would likely employ a financial advisor, the counterpart of an employment placement company, to help him find a worthwhile investment. Indeed, to an increasing degree, financial investment is passing into the hands of professional investors including managers of pension funds and mutual funds. These professional investors must find an outlet for the money that they are entrusted with.

An employee

An employee invests his capacity and ability in a company. Just as the financial investor has expectations, so an employee also has expectations that include the expectation of a fair return in pay for the work that he does, security of employment and a developing career. Similar to the investor he may elect at some time to receive lower pay so that he can advance later in life. Like the investor of money he can, by changing jobs, move his investment from one company to another. He can also move his investment by reducing his commitment to the work that he is asked to do and increasing his commitment to some activity outside the company, such as volunteer work, further study, local politics, or something similar.

Much of the work that is done in a company, particularly at the higher levels, requires fairly intense and continuous commitment. Without this, little can be accomplished. Unless he sees some satisfaction in what he is doing, an employee will not give this intense application. Yet the company grows and can satisfy the needs of the stockholder out of just such application and commitment. Like the stockholder the change of employment may not be easy to make. The employee may have to go to a recruitment firm for help in making the change.

If, therefore, we say that a company is in business to make a profit for the stockholders because otherwise they will withdraw their support and cause the company to decline, we should say also that a company is in business to satisfy employees' need to work, and if this need is not met the employees will withdraw their commitment and so in turn cause the company to decline.

The market

Yet a third force must be reckoned with: the market. The market represents the need that society has for the continued existence of the company. The market, like the stockholder and the employee, has its expectations. These are for a quality product at a reasonable price. The market will also balance short-term against long-term considerations in the same way that the employees and stockholders do. If the market does not feel that its needs are being met, then it will look for their satisfaction elsewhere. This is like saying that the market invests or commits its needs in a particular company in anticipation that these needs will be satisfied. If the company fails to provide that satisfaction, then commitment is withdrawn.

A certain amount of inertia or inelasticity exists within the market, as among stockholders and employees, that tends to resist change. A customer who has bought some equipment that requires specialized parts or supplies is, in a way, a captive market for the company selling the equipment. But the market does have flexibility and can change its commitment, and this change in itself can be an important cause for the decline of a company.

The market has become increasingly professional. Chain stores and supermarkets have replaced the corner stores and they employ professional buyers of goods, who wield considerable purchasing power. The automotive industry sells much of its product to fleet owners and to customers operating specialized equipment. In addition to this, with the rise of consumer protection and the various government bureaus dedicated to ensuring that the customer's rights are protected, the private market itself is becoming professionalized.

Commitment made by each of the three power holders

Each of these three — stockholders, employees, and market — makes its own kind of commitment to the company. The stockholder commits money; the employee commits his skills and know-how; the market commits need. Therefore each makes a commitment, and though these are different in kind, each is essential to the continued existence of a company.

Commitment is an act of dynamic unity or will, and the company arises out of it. Therefore companies arise out of the drive to unity of the market, employees, and stockholders. This is tantamount to saying that a company arises out of the urge to unity, or the will of the society of which that company is a part. Thus, *the fundamental reason for a company being a company is to be found in dynamic unity expressed as commitment to give satisfaction to society as a whole*, and not just to give a return on the stockholders' investment.

The stockholder is the channel through which society sanctions what the company wishes to do. Society says, "Yes, you may do that," when money is invested in a company. Perhaps the principal difference between a free and socialist economy is the mechanism by which this social assent or commitment is made. In a controlled economy, a central authority says, "Yes, you may come into business, you may start production on that." But a free economy society uses a more sensitive, subtler medium to give its consent. The stock exchange is an extremely sensitive instrument by which society is constantly making judgments on what is occurring in the industrial and commercial world. Wall Street may not be a very good judge if 'good' means having high ethical standards, but it is an extremely sensitive judge. It is very quick to register approval or disapproval for changes within a company and within society at large.

The market, through the purchase of products, also gives assent to a company. The assent of a stockholder is, "Yes, you may do that." The assent of the market is, "Yes, you may do that, and with this result, or for this reason." The employees also give assent when they say, "Yes, you may do this, and this is how it will be done and the quality it will have."

We can see, therefore, that the market answers the question, 'why?' The employees answer the 'how?' The stockholders decree 'that' a company will be. The interaction of these three gives rise to a system. I defined a system earlier as *a set of independent but mutually related terms*. The stockholder, the market, and the employee are independent, but they are mutually related. They exist as independent elements of a single unified will that emerges from societies common will to be. A company is therefore a unity, a whole; but this unity is expressed through the interaction of three independent forces. The company is therefore a composite and multidimensional whole,

Which of the three power holders is the most important?

If one stockholder holds a thousand shares while another holds but ten, then, as far as the company is concerned, the commitment of the first is more important than the commitment of the second. Similarly, if one customer purchases a thousand items and another customer but one, the commitment of the first is more important than the commitment of the second. Differences of more or less importance can occur along a given dimension, whether the stockholder, market or employee dimension; but it is pointless to ask which of the three dimensions is the most important one. Each makes its own legitimate contribution and each has its own legitimate expectation. Each strives to maximize its return from the company in which its commitment is invested. Each, therefore, strives to be the one cause of which the other two are consequences. To say that the stockholders are the most important and so consider the stockholders to be the cause of the company's activities — with the other two dimensions being the consequence — turns the system into an exploitive rather than an economic system.

When we talk about a 'company' we are dealing with a label, not with an entity, a thing. The incorporation of a company is simply a legal process by which these three forces are given a field on which to play. When saying that a company exists for this or that reason — say for making money for its investors — one should keep in mind that we are saying that the three forces are biased in that direction. Ideally the reason for a company's existence would be multivalent — serving all three dimensions— and not univalent — serving one dimension only. Later I shall introduce more 'dimensions' that make up a 'company': the suppliers, the general public, the government among others.

In the next chapter I shall go into more detail why I call these three forces a 'field'.

Notes

1   Kelly, *The Divine Right of Capital*, pp. 52–53.
2   *Ibid.*, p. 53.
3   Galbraith, *The New Industrial State*, p. 16.
4   *Ibid.*, p. 16.
5   Drucker, *The Age of Discontinuity*, p. 205.
6   Wilfred Brown, *Explorations in Management* (London: Heinemann, 1960).

CHAPTER ELEVEN

The Company as a Field

The three commitments of the stockholder, market, and employee can be looked upon as forces that make up the *field* of the company. The product arises out of the field, or *commitment space*, and the product provides a return to stockholder, employee, and market for the investment that each is making. The field is not a physical one such as a magnetic field; but it is not just a purely subjective field. This is why I called it a *commitment* space.

Apart from the basic requirement of thinking clearly, another reason for making the distinction between 'the company' and the 'field' is the following. Classical organization theory suggests that on the one hand there is 'the company' and on the other there is 'change'. One view states that change occurs in the company, or that change happens to the company, or yet again that the company undergoes change. Classical organization theory has its origin in the way we are taught to think, and according to this way of thinking, everything exists as a thing; the world is a thing filled with things. A company, from this point of view, is also a thing; it can change but only because of something else happening. What I am suggesting is that a company is not a thing: *it is the orderly expression of change*. The orderly expression of change occurs along three 'spatial' dimensions: horizontal, lateral, and vertical.

Let us consider a cobbler who makes shoes. Let us suppose that he takes on additional help to make shoes because of an increase in the amount of work he is called upon to do. When he does so his 'company' changes *laterally*. He and his helper work side by side; each completes a whole task cycle. If he then takes on someone to sell the shoes, his company changes horizontally along the task cycle. If he employs a number of people to do the work, and he no longer makes the shoes but supervises others that do so, then his company has changed vertically. Lateral change is change in the relation of different departments, horizontal change is change in the way of carrying out specific task cycles, and vertical change means the addition or deletion of a level of supervision. The company's functions become increasingly more differenti-ated and complex. New systems, procedures, and understandings bring about new integrations or new orientation, and new wholes tend to be created within a company. These bring about horizontal and lateral changes. As the company grows, higher-level ideas are introduced, enabling it to encompass an increasing field of phenomena, which require higher levels of supervision. In this way it changes vertically.

Change, therefore, can occur at many different points within a company, but to see a company as *something* that is changing, rather than being an orderly process of change, means that a tendency to resist change is built into the very way we perceive and think about a company.

What could be called a 'cataclysmic' approach to reorganization is often adopted according to which a company is organized at a given time and then, through failure to adapt, it reaches a crisis, then reorga-nization becomes necessary, and the cycle is repeated. By regarding a company as a field, a dynamic system (or the orderly expression of change) open to its environment, having many dimensions, each of which in turn is the orderly expression of change, the cataclysmic approach can be replaced by a more dynamic approach based on growth, expansion and self-regulation.

On growth, expansion and self-regulation

In the corporate world growth commonly means but one thing: to get bigger, and most often even the meaning of bigger is limited to bigger profits. How often do we hear that a company had a good first, second, or third quarter meaning that its profits increased? But we do not hear that 3,000 employees of the company lost their jobs in that quarter and a whole community in which these employees lived and worked was devastated because the company closed down one of its plants. Success is equated with size, rationalized as economy of scale, and projected as a national faith through the G.N.P. index with conglomerates as the result. A balloon, as it is blown up, gets bigger — but this is not growth. It is simply expansion. As many a breathless and startled reveler has discovered, bigger is not always better. The capacity of the balloon does not grow, but its capacity is subjected to more and more demands. Expansion could therefore be seen as increasing the demand on the capacity of a single company dimension. Growth, on the other hand, means increasing the capacity of each of the dimensions, as well as increasing the demands that are made upon them.

Partial reorganization of a company brings about expansion or inte-

gration. Expansion occurs when those parts of the company that are reorganized increase their demands upon the rest of the system (for example,
a new sales drive). Integration comes about when the reorganization
makes it possible for different parts of the system to interact more easily
(for example, a work simplification program). Only total reorganization
can bring about growth. Without growth, the forces of differentiation and
integration become opposed in unresolved conflict, causing fragmenta-
tion, empire building, and eventually the decline of the company.

We can therefore differentiate three forms of orderly change that can
occur:

1 The change of integration, which we shall call self-regulation.
2 The change of expansion.
3 The change called growth.

I can now propose a specific definition of a company: *a multidimensional field of interacting forces capable of growth, expansion, and
self-regulation, with a product as its dynamic center.* A company, therefore, is not a thing, but a set of interacting forces. Any theory of
organization must be capable of reflecting a company's many facets, its
dynamism, and its basic orderliness. For example, when a company
organization is reviewed it must be looked upon as a whole, as a total
dynamic system.

The whole is a system and the word 'system' implies a *mutual relationship*: a system is a set of independent but mutually related elements,
processes or forces. I emphasize *mutual* relationship because the mutual
relationship is frequently ignored when organizations are reviewed.
When managers reorganize they often do not give enough attention to
how parts of the system are related in time or structure. Furthermore,
relatedness is something that is poorly understood. For example,
managers frequently write job descriptions in complete isolation from
other job descriptions, and even in isolation from what the company as
a whole is trying to accomplish. A salary administration system is often
put in without any real understanding of the company's overall organization. Although organization charts are drawn, they often ignore the
content of job descriptions. A gesture is sometimes made in the direction of relatedness and structure by putting dotted lines on the
organization chart, but these frequently serve to confuse rather than to
clarify the issue.

In addition to job descriptions and organization charts in a company,
there are other elements such as budgets, appraisal systems, systems for
introducing new products to the company, salary-administration

systems, long-range forecasts, management-development systems, goal-setting systems, data-processing systems, and management-information systems. All are developed independently with very little integration and frequently with an increasing despair on the part of those who are called upon to develop the systems, because they recognize how little relevance what they are doing has for the rest of the company. The increasing reliance on outside help from consultants can make this tendency worse if the consultants are not keenly aware that the company is a whole and not just a collection of departments and functions.

But, if we see the company as a field then we are encouraged to see it as a dynamic set of interacting forces, that is a set of forces changing through time. This tells us that the company is not a thing or simply a collection of things. Neither a thing nor a collection of things can grow. A thing can get bigger, but getting bigger is not necessarily growth. Things can be added to the collection, but growth can be considered to have taken place only when the interaction, the mutual relevance of these things is taken into account, and, furthermore, when these interactions increase both in number and in complexity.

The notion of a field allows for these interactions to be taken into account. This notion also allows for a qualitative understanding based on the notions of fitness, order, harmony, emergence, and balance, as well as an understanding of value in terms of levels. Furthermore, and perhaps this is the most important, when the company is seen as a dynamic field of forces in equilibrium, an orderly expression of change is possible.

We can grasp the notion of a field more readily if we no longer rely solely on the on/off dualistic thinking that is so familiar and that is so often considered to be the only legitimate way to think. Our understanding of corporate life is bedeviled by dualities and dichotomies, by 'either/ors': management/workers, staff/line, centralized/decentralized, skilled/unskilled, stockholders/employees. I am suggesting an alternative to this dualistic view, an alternative that will alleviate so much of the frustration, sense of futility, and indeed destructiveness that arises because of our present way of thinking.

The interaction of the three power groups to create a field

These three forces are not static. Each is in opposition to the others and yet each is dependent upon the others. Each is opposed because each seeks to maximize its returns: the customers seek to get the best possible bargain for their commitment — they will look for the best quality at the cheapest price; the employees will seek the best conditions in terms of

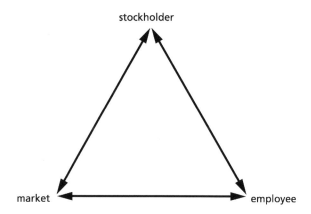

Figure 11. 1 The interaction of the three forces

pay and challenge; the stockholders will seek the most secure growth and best dividends. The customers are dependent upon the stockholders and employees, in the same way that the stockholders are dependent upon the employees and customers. *Each has an implicit contract with the other two.*

Because each is seeking to maximize its returns, each of the three power groups will tend to migrate to other companies unless some force of attraction holds them to a particular company. This pull from outside gives an outward direction, or centrifugal direction (from the center to the periphery) to the dynamism of the forces.

Dynamic tension within the field[1]

However, the forces are not just in competition — that is, they are not simply opposed to each other. They are also complementary: they mutually support each other. This will give a centering tendency, a countermanding centripetal (from the periphery to the center) force. If the center of attraction were absent a company could not stay in business even for a moment.

The centrifugal force comes from each wanting to maximize its returns in opposition to the others. This is not a conscious opposition, but because each wants to get as much as it can, and because at any one time only so much money is available, each necessarily opposes the others.

The centering tendency comes into being because each wants another kind of return (let us call it for the moment a 'centering' return) from the company. Employees do not only want more money; they also

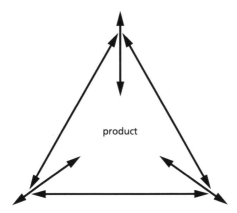

product

Figure 11. 2 Interacting forces

want challenge, recognition, and personal growth. Customers do not only want something that is cheap, they also want a good quality product that will last and that has pleasing features. Stockholders, too, do not only seek dividends, but also want to see their investment grow and some stockholders even want this to happen in an enterprise worthy of growth.

The centering tendency is realized in the product of the company. The product is the dynamic center that holds a company together and each of the forces collaborates to produce the product. The collaboration is not a conscious collaboration, but as each seeks to maximize its 'centering tendency', a product comes into being. The diagram can now be expanded.

Figure 11.2 shows a set of interacting centripetal and centrifugal forces. As we shall see later, the product counteracts the centrifugal exploding force; the organizational structure counteracts the centripetal, imploding tendency.

The field and creativity

If we refer back to Koestler's definition of creativity, a single idea in two or more mutually exclusive frames of reference, we will see that the field as I have defined it is a creative field. I said that each of the forces in the field seeks to maximize its returns. In other words the forces are three mutually incompatible frames of reference. The centripetal and centrifugal drives of the forces are also incompatible. The product is an idea in a form with a demand. Thus the 'idea' that makes creativity possible in the field of mutually exclusive demands and tendencies is the idea of the product. The product gives the field a *dynamic center*. As each of the three forces contributes to the production of the product, they are not only antagonistic to each other, they also co-operate with each other. As the product grows, in the way that I have defined growth, the company also grows.

The description of the field as centripetal and centrifugal is the description of a holon. A holon is 'Janus-faced'; that is, it has two faces, one looking inward and the other looking outward. It also has the characteristics of being both a whole and a part. A company is a holon. Its integrating, centripetal tendency enables it to survive; its expansive, centrifugal aspect fulfills its mission. As a whole it survives; as a part of a wider whole — the society within which the results of its actions are felt, it fulfills its mission. Its mission is to provide a meaningful outlet to the natural creativity of the employees, to give a return on investment to the stockholder, and to give a worthwhile product to the market.

The job of the president

The conflict and cooperation between the forces of the stockholder, employees and market do not operate on a conscious level, and so far I have pictured this conflict and cooperation as sets of 'blind' forces at work. They are forces operating in the dark and are really forces in potential. The job of the president allows them to meet in a conscious way. He does so in two ways: he balances as far as possible the claims of the three forces so that their commitment to the company continues. He also balances the survival and expressive needs of the company and, by doing so, he ensures a product is produced. Given that work is the exercise of

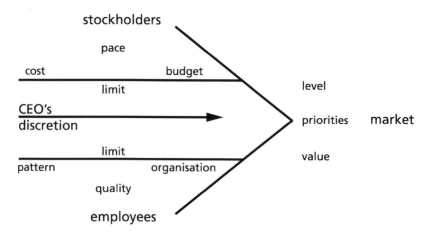

Figure 11. 3 President's job overlaid manager's job

discretion within limits to produce a result, a president's job is to satisfy the market within the limits provided by the stockholder and the employee, to satisfy the employees within the limits provided by the market and the stockholder, and to satisfy the stockholder within the limits provided by the market and the employees.

But, because he is the dynamic center of the company, the way that he carries out his function will also determine the *ethos* of the company. That is, he will determine it's fundamental and distinctive character, its value system — the spiritual, ethical, moral and legal context within which the field operates; and also the social system — the way that employees will interact with each other.

The limit that for the filing assistant's job was the time limit, the supervisor's job the cost limit, and the manager's job the limit imposed by the budget, for the President the same limit is the demands of the stockholders. What was the priority limit in these other jobs, for the President becomes the demands of the market as a whole, and what was the quality and organization limit for them, becomes, for the President, the demands of the employees.

Summary

In the Introduction I said that the structures underlying human nature, creativity, and work are isomorphic. In this chapter I have shown this same basic structure is the structure of a company and that its structure is therefore isomorphic with human nature, creativity, and work. By doing so I have shown how one can think about a company in an entirely new way.

We can now see a company as a *human* enterprise and not simply a financial one nor simply as a legal fiction. A company is not simply the result of a set of financial forces that somehow have come into being, and which are controlled by some mysterious abstract figures known under the collective name of 'Wall Street'. The current univalent view, based on this entirely abstract theory of corporate life, sees only one dimension of a company as important. The stockholder is looked upon as the reason for the company's existence, and the satisfaction of the stockholder as the main motive of the management of that company. The satisfaction of the needs of the other two dimensions thus is a consequence of the company making a profit.

Seeing the company as a human enterprise is not simply of value as a theory, it has immense ethical and practical consequences. Practically it shows how work can be organized in such a way that it will satisfy the manifold needs of those who invest in the company: the employees, stockholders and customers. Ethical conduct requires a sensitivity to the needs of the whole and not simply to one or more of its constituent parts; what I am saying about a company shows how such a whole can be understood as a field made up of mutually exclusive but mutually dependent dimensions.

Note
1   Kurt Lewin, ed., Dorwin Cartwright, *Field Theory in Social Science* (New York: Harper Torch Books, 1951). "Using the construction of a 'system in tension' for representing psychological needs definitely presupposes a field theory," p. 11.

CHAPTER TWELVE

On Task Cycles

The field of a company has a space-like quality; indeed I referred to the field as a commitment *space*. The three power groups exist simultaneously 'alongside' each other, so to say, in commitment space. We could refer to the field as *company as structure*. But a company is not only a structure; it is also a *process*. In company as process the investments of the power groups make *task cycles* possible, which occur in sequence: that is to say in a time-like way. A company can be looked at as an ambiguous space/time or structure/process continuum. The structure organization and process organization are not two separate organizations: they both involve the whole company and are not two halves of it. In the same way the young and old woman are not two separate illustrations. They involve the whole illustration and are not two halves of the illustration.

A task cycle: the atom of a company

A task cycle and a company are isomorphic. We can see that this is clearly so if we compare the self-employed cobbler with a large company, and realize that all that is done in the large company is also done in the one-man business. What the shoemaker does as one task among many other tasks, in a large company is done by a job, a department or even out-sourced to another company. For example, collecting money for the shoes he has made is just one task that the cobbler has to do, but in a large company a finance department would be required. Indeed some companies outsource the collection of money to another company entirely such as Visa or Master Card. What starts out as a task within a job may develop into a job, then a department, and finally may be subcontracted out to a company specializing in performing that one task. Many examples of this have occurred in the automotive industry. A task cycle is then quite clearly isomorphic with a company.

A task cycle is made up of sub-cycles or elements and in its turn is part of a larger, super cycle. The task cycle is the *atom* of the company.

A whole company finds its focus in each task cycle that is accomplished, and in turn is made up of all the task cycles that are occurring. The *hologram*, of which each small part contains the whole, is the perfect metaphor. A company itself is a whole ongoing task cycle and can be seen as such. Born of an idea, it grows as long as the idea is clearly perceived, and dies when the idea ceases to be a dynamic center. It is composed of many cycles and sub-cycles. Therefore to fully understand a company as process, what is meant by the expression *task cycle* must be well understood.

What is a task cycle?

Task cycles may be carried out by individuals (a typist typing a letter) or by the company as a whole (building an extension to the manufacturing plant). Both are task cycles. To help in further understanding the expression 'task cycle', consider again the work of a cobbler. When a cobbler makes a pair of shoes he first decides upon the shape, color, size, and style. He then gathers together the various materials needed to make the shoes and then produces them. He then puts them on display and eventually sells them to a customer. This is a task cycle.

In the above example we see that a task cycle goes through various stages: deciding which type of shoes to make, producing them, and selling them. These are three sub-cycles. The first sub-cycle is concerned with *developing* the product (PD) ; the second, with *processing* or manufacturing the product (PP); and the third, with *linking* the product to the customer (PL). The task cycle with its sub-cycles can be depicted as in Figure 12.1.

This analysis of a task cycle fits in with the definition of a product that I have given: an idea in a form with a demand. Product development coincides with the idea, product processing with the form, and product linking with the demand.

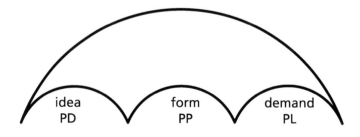

Figure 12.1 The task cycle

In developing the product, the idea is perceived. To use the cobbler once more as an example: he perceives the shoe. That is to say durability, flexibility, ease of putting on and taking off, color, shape, as well as cost and time available to do it, all have to be taken into account, all have to be related to the final product: a shoe. The cobbler takes all of these into account, and, through the product idea, he perceives the relations that these have to each other. If he fails to take something into account, say the size, the product will suffer. During the manufacturing, or processing phase, the idea will be put into a form and throughout production the idea will continue to act as a guide and a control. During the linking phase the customer will decide whether this shoe is what she wants. She asks herself whether the cobbler's idea of a shoe agrees with her idea of what her shoes should be like.

A task cycle is obviously not 'something'; we cannot point to it. If we walked around a factory floor, we would simply see a total ongoingness. In this ongoingness things are happening as a continuous process. This brings with it an important corollary: we cannot reach structure — that is the relation that elements have to each other — through the senses. Whoever says that he only believes what he sees, will not believe in structure. But the very timing of a task cycle, the interaction and integration, now at this level and now at that, of simultaneous but related task cycles, are the outcome of structure. This is why we have said that a company is a system: a set of elements in mutual relation. This mutual relation gives structure, or what could also be called organization, to the elements.

Task cycles in series and in parallel

In what I have said so far I have assumed that the task cycles within a company are in series, that is, one after the other. In the example of the cobbler, the product-development phase preceded the product-processing phase, and the product-linking phase followed. Such an example, though, is an abstraction for two reasons. A task cycle is not just a process, not just a sequence of events in time. It also has a structure given by the limits within which it occurs. The cobbler has on the one hand to bear in mind the price that he can get for the shoes and how much it will cost to make them. On the other hand, he has to bear in mind the skill that he has and the equipment he has available.

The second reason that the task cycle, as I have just described it, is an abstraction is that in the 'ongoingness of a company' tasks do not only occur one after another, they also occur simultaneously. Cycles not only occur in series, but also in parallel.

To take a stylized view of the automobile industry as an example, we can imagine that in a given year, say 2001, the cars for 2002 are being manufactured while plans for cars for 2003 will be developed, and the 2001 models are being sold.

Model year	2000	2001	2002	2003
2000	PL			
2001	PP	PL		
2002	PD	PP	PL	
2003		PD	PP	PL

The six dimensions of a company

We can now see that a company matures from its first beginnings as a single task cycle to become a fully mature company with six fully differentiated functions serving the six dimensions of the company: market (the Marketing department), the employee (Human Resources), the stockholder (Finance department), product development (R and D), product processing (Manufacturing plant) and product linking (Sales department).

The following diagrams illustrate this.

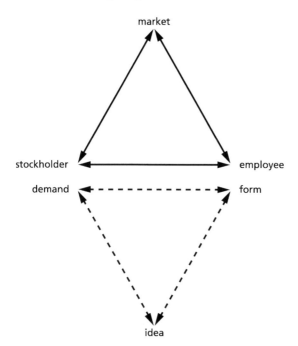

Figure 12. 2
Structure and
process fields

These two fields can be combined in two ways:

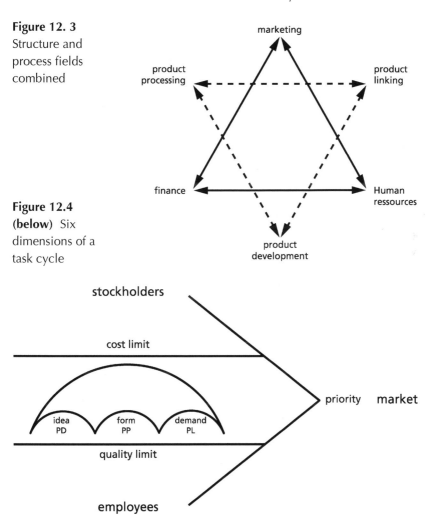

Figure 12. 3
Structure and
process fields
combined

Figure 12.4
(below) Six
dimensions of a
task cycle

These same six functions are present in both a job and in a department as well as in a task cycle. Thus these six dimensions are common to any productive process. Three of them are *structural*, and three *process*: the first three make the creative field possible, the second produces the product. We should not nevertheless believe that first the field is established and then the product produced. Rather, all six create the field and all six produce the product. The field is centered by an idea and this centering produces the product. A useful analogy for the emergence of the product is that of a crystal growing out of a gel. The seed of the crystal is the idea, the gel is the company as field; but the seed and the gel are made of the same ingredients.

The six processes have a number of different names. The following are the most obvious

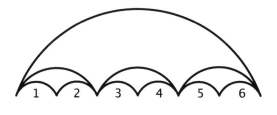

1 Identify need.
2 Design product.
3 Draw up action plan.
4 Manufacture product.
5 Inspect and evaluate product.
6 Link or sell product.

Figure 12.5 Names of six processes in task cycle

The first two cycles correspond to the marketing and product development; the second two correspond to organization/staffing and product processing, and are concerned with coalescing resources. The last two cycles correspond to finance and sales and are concerned with linking the product.

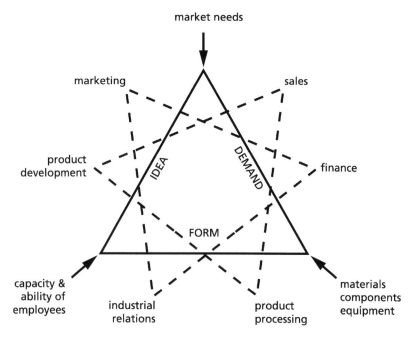

Figure 12.6 Total company field

An example

Let us return to the cobbler. He decides to set up business in a small town. First of all he travels around to determine whether there are other cobblers in town. While doing so he also checks out the styles of shoes that are available in the shoe stores. He buys some fashion magazines and talks with some people about the kinds of shoes that they like. He then locates a property where he can set up shop. He has some savings but by no means enough. He arranges with the bank for a line of credit. He then rents the property and buys machinery, tools, and raw materials. As he wants to conserve his capital he buys these on credit. He then opens his shop and a woman comes to buy some shoes. He discusses with her the style, color, size and material of the shoes and promises her that he will have them ready in a week's time. He makes a few drawings, then goes ahead, cuts out the leather shape and stitches it and so makes the shoes. At the end of the week the woman comes back tries the shoes on, pays for them and leaves.

All the dimensions of a company are present. He establishes his market, he arranges for investors — the bank and the manufacturers of the machinery — he himself is the employee dimension. He develops the product in conjunction with the market (the customer), processes it and links it.

Now suppose that business is really good and he now has six customers that want shoes. He will now have six task cycles to accomplish. He will probably require about three months to make all the shoes. He cannot now spend all of his time making them. He will have to start keeping accounts of who has paid, what materials he has available, what promises he has made. He will also have to order material and follow up on customers who have not paid. All this means that he will have to spend time ensuring an adequate cash flow, organizing his work and setting priorities.

Business continues to grow and so the cobbler takes on a few employees. He now spends less time making the shoes. He trains, trouble shoots, does quality control, and spends more time on the records. He now has to look ahead about 6–9 months to be sure that he has sufficient time to do all the work that requires being done. For example, he can put off ordering more machinery for a while, he will give a new employee a few months to settle in, he has to put off some decisions about enlarging the premises and so on.

As business continues to grow, he arranges for some friends to invest in his business, he extends the premises, gets new machinery, and employs more people. Now he needs someone to supervise the employees so that he is free to look further afield for markets, spend time with the investors to explain to them what he is doing and get their agreement, and plan a schedule for the work that has to be done. The supervisor that has taken his place will have to be able to plan ahead for about three months. As the company grows, so a supervision level is introduced. As a company grows further, additional levels are added.

A corollary to this growth is that as new levels are introduced so a longer *time span* is necessary to do the work of the higher levels. Time span means the length of time that a person needs to accomplish the work that he has to do. The higher the level of work, the longer the time-span that is necessary to do it. In the example that I gave above the cobbler started by having a time span of one week: it took one week to make the shoes. Then, with six customers, not only does the amount of work increase, but the length of time that it takes to do the work also increases. Because the cobbler now has to decide on priorities and to organize the flow of work in more complex ways, his level of work increases accordingly, and he now has a time span of three months in which to do the work. And so his level of work has increased. As a supervisor he has even more complex priorities, has to juggle more finance and organize an even greater degree of complexity and so the time necessary to accomplish this increases accordingly to about nine months. The following table illustrates this

Manager	. . .	9 months –15 months
Supervisor	. . .	3–9 months
Worker	. . .	1 week–3 months

The company environment

As a company grows so its interaction with and influence on the surrounding environment increases. Even as a single cobbler the 'company' has this interaction and influence, but it does not become significant until a company has reached a certain level of maturity. We must complete the picture of a company by including other forces with which it interacts and which it influences. These are often included in what are now called 'stakeholders', but it would be better to look upon them as additional dimensions of the company.

Each of these new dimensions is closely associated with one of the dimensions of the company field although each affects the whole company field.

The government and the finance dimension are closely associated.

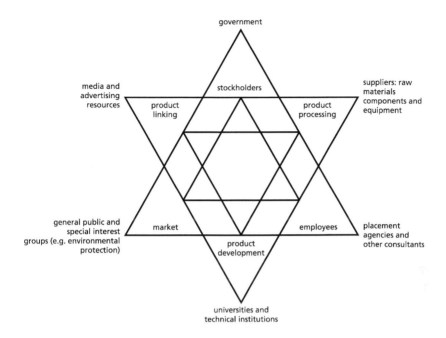

Figure 12.7 Environment of a company

The close association is clearly brought out in a socialist country where the stockholder dimension is the government. In a company that is large enough, a legal department will be employed to relate the company to this dimension.

Suppliers of components and equipment are closely associated with the product-processing dimension. This is obvious when a company subcontracts to an independent company the responsibility for manufacturing a component that previously was manufactured in-house. A Purchasing Department will often be responsible for the company's relation to this dimension.

Technical associations, institutions and universities, research and technical know-how are closely associated with the product development dimension. Universities provide valuable services in the form of research and consulting. Technical knowledge is also available through magazines, books, seminars, and the personal interaction of like-minded people. Most companies recognize the importance of allowing their managers to have the opportunity of visiting other companies, reading relevant publications and attending conferences. A librarian will often be employed to look after part of this dimension.

The general public is closely associated with the company's market.

This is borne out quite clearly in the struggle that often arises between the public relations group and the marketing group — particularly over the control of advertising that aims at reinforcing or modifying the company image. A Public Relations Department will be set up to deal with this dimension.

The media and advertising resources are closely associated with the sales function. They help to convert needs to demands by increasing people's willingness to pay for a product. The function of the sales group is to convert the ability to pay into a willingness to pay. An Advertising Department will have the responsibility for such work.

A company, through the organization and staffing department, will draw on employment placement agencies and consultants to help the company find employees with the capacity and ability necessary to do the work of the company.

Summary

A great deal of attention is given to, and energy expended upon, ethics in the business world. Much of this is but a band-aid on a system that needs major surgery. As long as the main motivation is 'to get the numbers' to increase share value at no matter what cost to the other dimensions, ethics will be given lip service at best, relegated to the garbage bin at the worst.

I said earlier that ethical conduct is based on thinking that is sensitive to the nuances of the situation, and this sensitivity comes out of a high tolerance for ambiguity and a keen awareness of wholeness and unity. Wholeness and unity must include the wider dimensions that I have indicated above. To see the company simply as a set of investors, who are interested in gambling with the company's stocks, is a completely unrealistic and abstract view in which ethics can play no part. A company is not separate from the society in which it finds itself any more than the Marketing department, or any other department, is separate from the company in which it finds itself. A company is not even a part of the society. It is one way that society functions: it is one dimension, to use a familiar term, of society.

Seeing all the company dimensions — those that I have introduced in this chapter as well as those that I introduced earlier — as dimensions, and not as resources to be used by one dimension of the company (i.e. a set of anonymous investors), will give a firm foundation on which to develop a secure and realistic code of ethics.

CHAPTER THIRTEEN

Types of Work

In the Introduction I said that we cannot think intelligently about many of the questions concerning the corporate system because we simply do not have an adequate language. Not only is it inadequate because words such as corporation, profit, and work are not clearly defined, language is also inadequate because, for example, in the case of the word 'work' we have only one word that refers to a complex field. This inadequacy leads us to see work as a homogenous kind of activity, which can make for endless difficulties.

Edmund Carpenter,[1] when writing about the Inuit language, pointed out that the Inuits have many different words to describe snow. This is so because snow is so important to them. He said, "Language is the principal tool with which the Inuit make the natural world a human world. They use many words for snow, which permit fine distinctions, not simply because they are much concerned with snow, but because snow takes its form from the actions in which it participates: sledging, falling, igloo building, blowing. These distinctions are possible only when experienced in a meaningful context. The Inuit *brings different kinds of snow into existence* as they experience their environment and speak. The words do not label something already there." (my emphasis)

Just as Inuit bring different kinds of snow into existence as they talk about it within different contexts, so different kinds of work can be brought into the industrial West by seeing work within different contexts. Nine different types of work that are done within a company can be brought into existence in this way. Three of these depend on the kind of commitment that the job occupant makes, and six depend on the kind of work that the job requires to be done. Because we have not distinguished these differences our understanding is that much the poorer, and our actions to that extent less reliable.

Commitment

The three types of work depend upon the kind of commitment that the job calls for. These are 'employment', 'entrepreneurial', and 'good neighbor work'.

Employment work

Employment work is the work we do for pay and fulfillment. This work enables the company to survive. Without it a company cannot continue to exist. The manager of a particular job decides what product it should produce and ensures that the product idea can satisfy a need that the company has. He also ensures that the three limits — cost, quality and priority — are set, and that these limits are adjusted to each other. The job occupant doing employment work must, within these limits, realize the maximum potential of the product idea. He does so by finding different ways of expressing the product idea. The product is therefore variable within limits.

Entrepreneurial work

The entrepreneur opens up new markets by perceiving a new product idea, and then producing and selling the product. Because he does something new and untried, he takes a risk that someone who is doing employment work, and who therefore has a given product idea and a known and ready-made market for it, does not take. Someone doing employment work can be shown to be inadequate because his work does not meet required standards. The entrepreneur can also be shown to be inadequate in this way, but he can also commit himself to the wrong idea and so proven wrong.

An employee can also perform entrepreneurial work within the context of his company. To do so, he identifies a need within the company itself, not within society. This need would be one that up till then had not been recognized by the company. He must also perceive a product idea that will satisfy that need, generate a demand for the product, and create the product.

An example of entrepreneurial work within a company is the following. As a salary administrator I was given the job of setting pay scales for the employees of the company. I recognized that in order to set these up a thorough review of the company organization was first necessary. This reorganization, in turn, meant that a new understanding about organization had to be made known to the managers of the company. To introduce the new organizational understanding and planning a completely new kind of job, that of organization administrator, had to be set up. For a while, until the President sanctioned what I was doing, I was no longer doing just employment work — that of salary administrator — for which I had been employed. I had established a new product idea and had moved out of the limits imposed by my manager. Furthermore, my manager could not legitimately sanction my action. If he had done so then he too would have joined me as a partner in my entrepreneurial activity.

If the entrepreneur's product idea is of a sufficiently high level, the company may have to be re-aligned to produce it. Therefore, the higher the level of the product, the higher the level of management that must be persuaded to adopt the idea; and the consequences, if the idea turns out to be a dud, become more acute. To be an entrepreneur, someone must 'stick his neck out'. Furthermore, as he must also continue to fulfill the requirements of his employment work, he must either be able to organize that work well so that he has spare time to pursue entrepreneurial work, or he must do the latter work in his own time.

Some companies that appreciate the value of new ideas have tried to encourage their development by setting up suggestion boxes. Suggestion boxes, though, often fail because new ideas are not enough; one must be willing to expose oneself to a potentially hostile environment to realize the idea. Thus entrepreneurial work requires commitment that is different to that of employment work. An employee who is prepared to risk his reputation, who is willing to invest time and energy in the realization of an idea, and who in any case has the creativity necessary to perceive the idea, is highly committed to ensuring that the idea is introduced.

Entrepreneurial work, therefore, is work that potentially sets up new patterns and new possibilities within the company because it responds to a new need that the company has, whereas employment work satisfies an already existing need.

Good neighbor work

Good neighbor work, like employment work, is work for which a need already exists; it is not employment work because one does not get paid for doing it. We do this kind of work because it is intrinsically interesting; doing it is its own reward. Work as a volunteer — church work, charitable work, or work promoting junior sports — is an example of good neighbor work.

We can also do good neighbor work in a company. One kind of good neighbor work that is important within a company is assisting and advising others. Each job must have its own reason for being. Each job serves a specific need and has a specific product idea that is of value to the organization as a whole. Once we realize this then it becomes obvious that advice and assistance are given outside the range of employment work.

Job descriptions of employment work often include words like 'advise', 'assist', and 'collaborate with'. These create confusion because the occupants of jobs described in this way are paid to give advice to others. They are expected to give it and others therefore are expected to take it, or at least give the impression of taking it. Advice, though, is only advice if one can freely accept or reject it. Advice, therefore, can only be sought; it cannot be imposed.

The word 'advice' comes from the Latin *ad videre*, 'to see'. To produce a product one must perceive the idea. The one who perceives the idea is the one who produces the product. Perceiving the idea is a sub-cycle of a task cycle. If jobs are linked according to product, the linking will not create a problem. But if jobs are linked according to advice, then a conflict is inevitable, as the two job occupants may well perceive different product ideas within the same field.

If I am paid to give advice to others, I will necessarily do all in my power to get others to accept it. If others refuse to do so, then I will feel that my livelihood is threatened, and to an increasing degree I will concentrate on selling myself and tailoring my advice to meet my client's level of acceptance, rather than to meeting the needs of the situation.

I may also have friends in high places, and I can therefore force my advice on others. Those who have to receive my advice will resent doing so and resent my efforts to make them accept it. They will resist receiving it and so will avoid calling for it. Sometimes they may truly need advice and assistance; they may need someone with more experience or know-how to help them solve a problem. But they hesitate to call for advice, as they know from previous experience that they are simply calling for someone to take over the very work they are paid to do. Therefore, they in turn will feel that their livelihood is threatened.

A break down in communications is likely to arise as a consequence. Jobs will develop shells around themselves, and good neighbor work will wither. The company structure may start to come apart and senior management may feel that they have to use power to hold the company together. They may well then threaten overtly or covertly those who are defending their right to work, and so these people will likely withdraw causing the tempo of disintegration to increase.

By definition, we are not paid to do good neighbor work: doing it is reward enough, and people will want to do it for its own sake. A well-organized company that has employees that are secure in their employment work will also have employees willing to advise and assist others, as well as employees willing to seek advice from others. It would, therefore, be a well-integrated company and would suffer relatively few communication problems. Furthermore, the more good neighbor work that is done, the more interesting the company becomes, and the more the employees enjoy working for it.

The ill effects of poor language

If we have but one word to refer to three quite different kinds of work we will compound those three different kinds in a confused understanding. This confusion will cause us to make poor decisions. For example, employment work is paid for by a wage or salary. Pay grades are established and pay increases are given to reward this kind of work. Yet pay increases are sometimes given for entrepreneurial work and more frequently for good neighbor work — that is for giving advice. Entrepreneurial work should be paid for in the long run by promotion. Someone who is capable of entrepreneurial work is frequently capable of being promoted. In the short run, it should be paid for by a bonus. Good neighbor work should not be paid for by increases within the pay grade because, if an increase is given as a reward for doing it, it becomes employment work with the adverse effects that I described above. However, the astute administrator will not ignore the fact that an employee performs good neighbor work because, like all work, it is best done in the light of recognition. But the administrator will not commit the blunder of 'merit' rating an employee on 'co-operation' or 'loyalty'. Cooperativeness and loyalty, good neighbor work in fact, cannot be bought, but this is no reason for it not being rewarded.

Entrepreneurial work causes conflict. It must do so. People move out of their job structure and move into the job structure of others. These others resent interlopers, and this work therefore can become a threat to the integration of a company. A company that has too many entrepreneurs will suffer considerable conflict. Entrepreneurs rock the boat and they also rock one another. Poorly organized companies cannot tolerate such conflict and suppress the entrepreneur. If, on the other hand, the manager of an entrepreneur recognizes that entrepreneurial work is different from employment work, that it does mean crossing boundaries, that it does mean innovation and change and all that change implies, then he will diagnose the conflict correctly and instead of looking for ways to suppress it and to punish the person responsible for causing it, he will seek ways to give that conflict constructive channels of expression, channels that enable the potential in the situation to be realized.

The basis of a company structure is therefore well-organized employment work because this generates the willingness to engage in good neighbor work, which, in turn creates a climate for entrepreneurial work. Although entrepreneurial work and good neighbor work are opposites they are reconciled by employment work. Good neighbor work enables the company to acquire a natural self-regulation, while entrepreneurial work enables the company to expand naturally.

Work that includes integration as well as expansion enables the company to grow. Entrepreneurial work brings new patterns, new possibilities, to come into focus; good neighbor work helps to ensure that these are not seen as threats; employment work brings these two tendencies together. By seeing that these three types of work are quite different, have quite different motivations, and lead to quite different organizational results, a climate can be generated in the company that will allow all three to find expression.

Structure

Three other kinds of work can be identified, and they concern the 'structural' aspect of an organization. They are 'product', 'integration', and 'control' work.

Product work

Product work is the work for which the job was set up. Generally speaking, when people think about work, they think about employment work of the product kind. If you ask a person what he does, he will answer by saying that he is a comptroller, budget analyst, market-research analyst, display artist, and so on. This is employment-product work. A job is set up to produce a product, and product work produces it.

Integration work

Integration work is concerned with the limits within which the product is produced. An employee must ensure that the structure within which his product work is carried on is maintained. Unless he does so he will waste a lot of energy. Examples of integration work are: budget preparation, reviewing the salaries of subordinates, complying with government regulations, conforming to the requirements of company policies. Integration work will also include ensuring that all employees at all levels are trained so they can do their work

One has to give energy and time to integration work, and one diverts this energy and time from producing the product of the job. As managers are frequently judged in terms of the product work they do, and not in terms of integration work, they often consider integration work a waste of time and frequently neglect doing it.

Control work

Control work aligns the results obtained with what is required by the higher levels of the system, that is, eventually, the company as a whole. It includes matching resources committed to results obtained. Without adequate control work the president cannot fulfill his function of balancing the forces at work within a company. Managing by objectives is one way to do this. Even so, so much emphasis is given to the belief that the best, simplest, or even the only objective of a company is to make a financial profit, that financial objectives and financial controls, 'the bottom line', so far outstrip the availability of other types of control that these financial control devices can cause major distortions within a company. It is as though one attempted to control a horse by blinding it, and heaving on one rein only.

Product, integration, and control work are quite different. If, for the moment we look upon the job as a holon, these three can be recognized in the following ways: Product work represents the assertive mode of the job, integration work maintains the integrity of the job, and control work is required to maintain the integrity of the higher system of which the job is a part.

These three types of work operate along three different dimensions of a company. Product work occurs along the horizontal dimension, integration work occurs across the lateral dimension, while control work occurs in the vertical dimension. Many managers believe that work flows from the president, through higher levels of management, through lower levels and so to the shop floor, but we can see that work can also, and should, flow horizontally and also laterally.

Because many managers do not recognize the complexity of the word 'work', they have difficulty in delegating work and this difficulty is clearly expressed in many job descriptions, which are, or should be, the principle means of job delegation. Because of this difficulty they cannot give their subordinates freedom to act. Furthermore, because they delegate work badly they lack objective criteria by which to judge their subordinate's performance. These criteria flow naturally from well-delegated work. Managers tend therefore to judge a subordinate according to the subordinate's *behavior* and not his performance. Such a tendency is reinforced by job descriptions being frequently behavior-oriented and not results-oriented.

Process

We should now consider the last three kinds of work, which correspond to the process dimensions of a company. These are: on-going, project, and flux work.

Ongoing work

Ongoing work recurs and is both predictable and cyclic. Employment work of the product, ongoing, kind is that work which is the dominant 'import/conversion/export process' and is that process by which the primary work of a company is done. This is so both for a company and for a job. Most people when they think about work in a company have a vague notion of this kind of work. Employment-product-ongoing work is best represented by a multidimensional matrix and cannot in any way be represented by a single line from the board of directors down to the 'rank and file.' This 'univalent' view is an oversimplification that turns the concrete complexity of the work being done into a meaningless abstraction and makes the 'bottom line' the only criterion by which a company's performance is judged.

The work of a company has many interacting, ongoing cycles. For example, a gas utility has the following kind of ongoing cycles: gas systems plans are drawn up, pipelines constructed, inspections made for leaks, and maintenance work performed on the pipe. After a number of years the network of pipes is removed from the ground, new systems are drawn up. Other parallel cycles occur by which gas is purchased, received from other companies, fed into the system, regulated, and passed through meters. Meters are read, customers billed, and cash received, banked, and accounted. All of this is done while employees are being recruited, screened, trained, promoted, paid, and reviewed.

Some of these cycles are short while others are long, but all the cycles are similar in being predictable, and they are all interconnected. Furthermore, ongoing work is self-sustaining, that is, feedback from ongoing work is part of the input for future ongoing work. Because of ongoing work, a company endures.

Flux work

Flux occurs around the ongoing cycles. Flux can be compared to noise or static in a communication system. It is unpredictable, non-cyclic, and entropic — it uses up potential in the system. Examples of flux abound: the missing file, the sick employee, the accident, the unforeseen result, the failure of another part of the system to operate, the crashing computer and unnecessary e-mails. Murphy's law "what can go wrong will go wrong" is the law underlying flux generation. Flux work aims at suppressing the flux, or neutralizing its ill effects.

Frequently managers think of flux work as being their main concern. As long as they are putting out fires, attending meetings, and getting ready for the next problem, they feel that they are working. Flux can reach a point at which the system begins to break down. Yet, one must not infer that flux is only bad. The ongoing cycles draw their raw material for growth from flux.

The external environment is one of the principal sources for flux. The customer may be asked, "Please return this stub with your payment " but the payment nevertheless comes in without the stub. The customer is not perverse; she is simply not part of that system. She simply does not care whether the system succeeds or fails. So whereas the assistant should handle many payments, she is held up searching for the account information of this one customer.

Unions also are a source of flux and so are stockholders. Some union officials see the product of their jobs as generation of sufficient flux to stop the system. Furthermore, many individual employees feel that they have won if in some way they have beaten the system. Stockholders can also generate flux. A phone call or letter is received "I am a stockholder of your company . . ." and this says implicitly, "I do not care whether your systems must stop, bend or break, but I must get what I want."

Nevertheless, all flux is not generated from outside, and an organization itself can be set up as a flux generator. Two parts of an organization can be at odds with each other and in this way they generate flux, as does the manager who does not use a system properly, who does not follow the normal communication lines, or who mislays reports. The greatest internal flux generator within a company must surely be what is sometimes called the *staff/line* organization in which staff are considered to be those that give advice, and line are those that must receive the advice.

Project work

In order to combat flux on a more constructive basis than simply suppressing it through flux work, many companies have taken to setting up projects. Some project work scoops up flux and turns it into ongoing work, thus raising the level of that ongoing work. Projects are set up to achieve a specific objective, and when that has been done the project is either disbanded and project work comes to a halt, or a new project is defined. Project work is a single-cycle task — although that cycle may be broken down into a set of sub-cycles — and has therefore a limited life span. Project work is parasitical upon the ongoing cycles of a company and only a limited number of projects can be undertaken at one time. This is quite obvious when one considers that employees most frequently made available for project work would otherwise be doing ongoing work.

Because the product of a project is often clearly defined, and the limits clearly set, and because it goes on apart from the rest of the company's activity, this kind of work is the easiest to organize and is often the most pleasant to do. Some companies only have project work. NASA when getting a man on the moon was an extreme example. Getting a man on the moon was a one-time project. The organization of NASA would have had this clearly defined goal. The goal had also clearly defined time and budget limits, and the task cycle would have been distinctly divided into product development, product processing and product linking phases. We must bear in mind that the kind of organization that NASA developed in order to accomplish its goal would not be suitable for a company whose work is almost entirely employment work of the product-ongoing, kind.

Job descriptions

The importance of distinguishing between ongoing, project, and flux work that is done within a company is obvious when one writes a job description. In writing a job description one should concentrate upon the product-ongoing cycle and ensure that it is clearly and adequately described. By doing this, the hard skeleton of the company is established, with the main employment-product-ongoing cycle forming the backbone. Only in the ongoing cycles can the true pattern of an organization be discerned, and by concentrating upon these one can set down a complete picture of the company.

When writing a job description, managers who fail to distinguish between different types of work when writing job descriptions, put down what comes to their mind with no way of knowing whether what they have written is complete. Furthermore, by not recognizing the basic underlying pattern, these managers fail to simplify the job description and so fail to avoid duplication. They often write what is uppermost in their minds. Another person, for example, the job occupant, reading the description will likely find the whole thing incomprehensible, or will get quite a different picture of the job to what was intended, and this alone can be the beginning of many problems. We should not be surprised therefore if we find that most job descriptions are put away and forgotten after they have been written. Few are sufficiently well written that they can be used as instruments in work allocation, work review, salary administration or training,

Let me sum up what I have said so far with the following diagram:

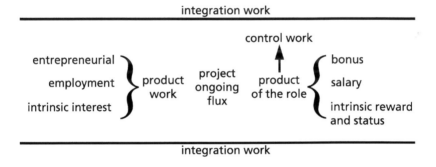

Figure 13.1 Types of work

Note

1   Edmund Carpenter, "Image Making in Arctic Art," *Sign, Image and Symbol* (New York: Braziller, 1966), p. 208.

CHAPTER FOURTEEN

Conflict and Growth

The company as a field under tension

The forces within the company field are under tension because they are legitimately at odds with each other, and so a situation exists that is ripe for conflict. But conflict is necessary for creativity to occur. Creativity arises when a single idea arises within two or more incompatible frames of reference. We could just as well use the word 'conflicting' instead of 'incompatible'. Struggle, difficulty, obstacles are necessary for growth to take place, both for an individual and for a company.

When conflict breaks out in a company it sometimes erupts as hostility, and the manager in whose department it occurs most often believes that it comes from conflict of personalities. Only one form of conflict has been institutionalized: the labor/management conflict; most others are seen as originating from the personalities of individuals.

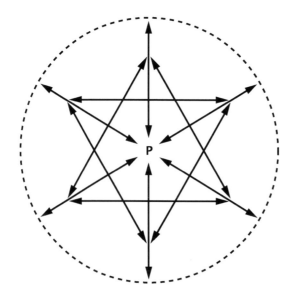

Figure 14 1 Company field under tension

According to this belief, organizational problems and conflict develop because people have different life experiences and so see, feel, and appraise things more or less differently. Conflict, stress, and negative relationships are seen to be the inevitable product. While this is true to some degree, it should not be inferred that conflict only arises from differing personalities.

Productive and non-productive conflict

Productive conflict comes from the nature of organization itself. One could say that each department seeks to maximize 'its own return' which creates tension and, possibly, conflict. We have also seen that entrepreneurial work may well generate conflict of a productive kind. Non-productive conflict arises either through poorly delegated work (such conflict often erupts as turf wars) or through personality clashes; the latter is probably much less frequent than most managers would believe.

Because in larger companies each of the six functions — the three structure functions and the three process functions — are most often delegated to a separate manager, productive conflict can arise. One will often see this in interdepartmental meetings where each manager sees the company product from the perspective of his own department. He is correct in doing so because that is what he is paid to do. Once this is recognized, instead of trying to dampen such conflict when it arises, some method should be devised to channel it creatively.

In their article *What you don't know about making business decisions*[1] the authors, David A. Garvin and Michael A. Roberto, point out that the decision making process involving creative conflict is not just a single event, but is an ongoing process, one that can continue for weeks, months and even years. As they say, it is "fraught with power play and politics." A group has two different ways of coming to a decision, ways that Garvin and Roberto call *advocacy* and *alternatives*. When group members use the way of advocacy each comes with a mindset that he is unwilling to change, and so will automatically reject alternatives. He looks upon the decision making process as a contest and has the underlying assumption that the best solution will come from a trial of strength.

The group that uses the alternatives way does not suppress conflict but encourages dissent. As Garvin and Roberto say, "conflict may be intense but it is rarely personal." Instead of trying to assert one solution over another, the aim of the group members is to seek to air all possible solutions and then, through frank discussion, come to a decision.

The important point that the authors make is that conflict is not necessarily undesirable, but that, on the contrary, working through conflict is part of the decision making process. They also point out that two other ways of looking at conflict are possible: *affective* and *cognitive*. Affective conflict would be dominated by emotional reactions and attacks on the personality; cognitive conflict would be a battle of ideas in which no one would win or lose, but a new idea which incorporates the best of the ideas would arise.

Executives at the upper levels tend to avoid open confrontation and conflict, and they are often unaware of ways by which to obtain genuine employee commitment to the organization. This leads to a higher proportion of conforming, mistrust, antagonism, defensiveness, closedness, than of individuality, trust, concern and openness. Not wanting to face up to the conflict inherent in work delegation, they often resort to exhorting subordinates to "think of the well-being of the company as a whole", or else insist that "we are all members of one great team and therefore should be willing to suppress our individual differences". This is solving conflict in a non-creative way. Employees who try to realize the full potential inherent in their position within such an environment — they are invariably the most conscientious people with the greatest integrity — are frowned upon. They, in turn, become guilt-ridden because they cannot fit in and equally guilt-ridden because they are forced to stand by while valuable potential is lost.

For a variety of reasons, some of which are perfectly valid, pure delegation is rarely made. By pure delegation I mean delegation in which the product and the limits within which it must be produced are clearly stated and assigned to one person. Jobs are often split, and overlaps, duplications, and omissions occur. These can bring about non-productive conflict. Because the framework does not allow for desirable conflict, because many managers have been trained to believe that all anxiety is neurotic, that human beings stop growing at about the age of sixteen, and because they are imbued with the either/or logic, conflict is suppressed.

Instead of suppressing conflicts, specific channels should be created to make productive conflict explicit, and methods set up by which to resolve it. Without these channels managers are apt to deal with conflict as flux work generated by personality conflicts, but this time resent it as wasted time. Just as flux work can be dealt with in an organized way, so creative conflict can be dealt with systematically. With controlled conflict, growth is possible. Unresolved conflict, on the other hand, will lead to frustration and hostility, which in turn will tend to emphasize individual differences, personality defects, and so bring to the fore interpersonal hostility.

Fear of conflict and poor organization

The fear of conflict itself is one of the major causes of poor organization. Through refusing to face and reconcile conflict in a creative way, many managers subsume jobs and tasks under departmental heads that functionally should not exist in those departments. Sales and marketing are often found under the same heading, although they are obviously looking at the customer from two entirely different points of view. The successful marketing manager has a completely different outlook from the successful sales manager. By combining these two functions into one department, either the long-range strategy of the entire company could be subjugated to immediate sales programs, or alternatively, sales programs could be made impossibly difficult through a lack of concreteness and definiteness.

Engineering or product design is sometimes subsumed under marketing in order to ensure that product development does not get 'out of line' with the needs of the customer. Whereas marketing is concerned with the integrating function, with how the resources of the company as a whole can be used, the engineering function is more concerned with the immediate task of realizing the potential of an existing product.

Two 'sins' are committed in life: the sin of commission — doing what is done badly, and the sin of omission — not doing what needs to be done. The more conflict is suppressed, the greater the chances are that what is being done will be done with the minimum of disruption, argument, and delay; but, on the other hand, the greater the chances are that more will be left out, more will be left undone. Trade-offs will be made that should never have been made, which in the end will mean slower growth for the company. Fewer ideas will be generated, and the company will tend to conform to what it has done in the past rather than develop new ways of doing things for the future.

Tension and levels of work

We could envisage a company as a center and a surrounding field. The center is the point of maximum *intrinsic tension*, and this tension is reduced as the periphery is approached. By intrinsic tension I mean tension that arises out of the dilemmas and ambiguities that are intrinsic to the job, not the subjective tension that someone might feel when doing it. The greater the intrinsic tension in the field, the higher the level of work that is necessary, and so a natural hierarchy emerges. Ambiguities become more pressing as one ascends the hierarchy. The intrinsic tension also increases because as one ascends the hierarchy, longer time spans elapse between the perception of an idea and its realization as a product. This longer time span means that a manager is required to be able to operate within a wider 'now' or present time than someone who is operating at a lower level of time span. If one does higher level work, it does not mean that one does more work, or even more important work. To do higher level work means to resolve higher levels of tension, generated by ambiguities and dilemmas, through product-oriented perception and activity.

The concept of job enrichment that has had a checkered career in industry is based on the fact that different levels of work exist in a company. The level of work given to an employee must offer some kind of challenge. Frequently, though, managers will give more work of the same, or even lower level in the mistaken notion that job loading is the same as job enrichment. Job enrichment only occurs when the job gives increased challenge to the employee; that is, when it provides creative tension of a higher level.

As we saw when discussing the growth of the cobbler's company, as a company grows so higher levels of work appear; thus higher levels of discretion are called for, which in turn call for higher levels of capacity from the people occupying the jobs. We saw also that one of the dimensions of a level of work is the time span of discretion required. The late Elliott Jaques pioneered this concept and spent his life trying to make it known. Time span, he said, was the length of time between the start of a task cycle and its review on completion. My own impression of the concept of time span of discretion is that it is extremely difficult, if not often impossible, to apply, but it is a wonderful way to think about organization and it makes a great deal more sense than anything else that I have read in management literature on organization.

The WCP Configuration

One of the principles derived from the notion of levels of work germane to our present concern with conflict, is what Jaques called the WCP equilibrium. **W** *is level of work,* **C** *is level of capacity required to do the work,* and **P** *is level of payment made in return for the work that is done.* Although ideally these three should be in equilibrium, they rarely are, and different configurations are possible any of which can generate confusion, chaos and conflict in a company. For example

W

C

P

would indicate a situation in which the level of work is above the level of capacity of the person occupying the job, but he is being underpaid for doing it. Suppose a manger whose WCP configuration is

P

W

C

who has a subordinate working for him who has a configuration

C

W

P

The manager is being over paid for the level of work that he is required to do, but the level of work is beyond his capacity to do it. His subordinate on the other hand has too much capacity for the level of work he is required to do. In any case the work level is underpaid. The manager would probably feel extremely insecure while his subordinate would feel frustrated and angry. As Jaques pointed out, and other researchers have confirmed, we have an innate sense of fairness, and when that sense is violated we suffer what Leon Festinger called *cognitive dissonance*[2] that can range all the way from the sense of unease to a sense of outrage.

Because the level of work is too high the manager will concentrate on what he can do, and that would mean that he would concentrate on lower level work. He would want to hoard that work to justify the pay he is getting, and he would probably do it meticulously. He would probably become defensive and sensitive to criticism, or else adept in PR and creating smoke screens. No doubt he would stay late and make a great show of taking work home. He would be reluctant to go on vacation for fear that someone who temporarily takes his place would realize what he had been up to.

His subordinate on the other hand would feel under worked and would look around for additional work to do. Because his manager would leave a good deal of his work unattended, the subordinate would possibly move in to take up the slack. He would no longer occupy a subordinate job. His manager would likely resent him; the manager would feel he was trying to steal his job. He could well see the subordinate as pushy and ambitious. The subordinate would harbor considerable resentment because of the poor pay that he was receiving, and probably blame his manager for not going to bat for him, something the manager dare not do because he would not want to attract attention to himself. When time comes around for performance rating he would give his subordinate a poor rating on co-operation, emotional maturity, and attention to detail.

I am not saying that this would have to be the outcome. However, we can see whatever the outcome, it would not be a healthy one. Perhaps you would care to envisage different WCP configurations and build up your own scenarios. You could then match those scenarios to your work place and see whether any of them clarify what goes on there. Most likely you will find that what is often diagnosed as a personality problem may well be a lack of WCP equilibrium. This suggests that before a company starts worrying about leadership and leadership styles, it should first address such organizational problems as those illustrated by the WCP equilibrium.

Level of work and span of control

Level of work, and its connection with conflict and tension, show up in another area — that of span of control. Although fewer people are paying the concept the attention that it once commanded, nevertheless some of its implications must be considered. The logic is that if a manager has 'too many' subordinates answering to him, then he should appoint a manager between him and some or all of these subordinates, and thus have fewer direct subordinates. However, the level of work of the employees reporting to the newly appointed manager would be lowered as a consequence because the resolution of dilemmas inherent in the situation that they were formerly expected to resolve now becomes the responsibility of the new manager, and the employees will experience a decrease in challenge.

A company has an optimum number of levels[3] and this number is related to the tension gradient in the field. The number is also likely to be fewer than the number frequently found in companies, because organizing is often confused with dividing the spoils, and managerial positions are sometimes created as sinecures to give comfort to their incumbents rather than results to the company. But even so the aversion to the hierarchy that one often finds when talking about organization is entirely misplaced. The aversion should be directed towards unnecessary levels.

A managerial job having task cycles requiring a time span of a year could comfortably have jobs of four to six months reporting to it — not longer or shorter. If the jobs do have longer time spans, unnecessary conflict is certain to occur; if shorter, then the manager will find that he is called upon to attend to detail of a level that is too low to maintain his interest.

Difference between growth and expansion

This gives me an opportunity to clarify further the difference between growth and expansion. Growth is an increase in capacity to take on higher-level work; expansion is the ability for a given capacity to do more work. Growth is related to job enrichment, and expansion to job loading. Both companies and individuals can therefore grow. Given that a company is operating with an optimum number of levels of management, it will grow through the addition of a level of management.

A level-three company has three legitimate levels of management,

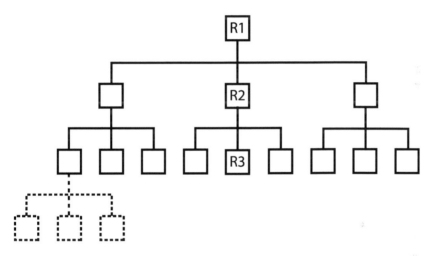

Figure 14.2 Levels and span

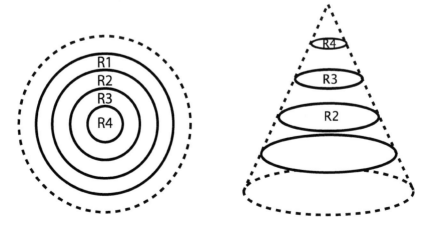

Figure 14.3 Levels

and it could grow to a level four company. The level-three company expresses a lower level idea through its product than the idea that a level-four company expresses through its product. This means that the task cycle designed to produce the product will be longer in the case of the level-four company than in the level three. Specifically, this will mean that whereas the president of a level-three company has a time span of two or three years, the president of a level-four company will have a time span of about five to seven years. Furthermore the company will require about six managers reporting to the president who have time spans of the level that the president had when the company was operating at optimum as a level-three company. Growth in a company would then be growth along all dimensions, whereas expansion is simply along one. The company organization chart is usually shown as a triangular-shaped structure (figure 14.2). Perhaps it would be better regarded as a cone (Fig, 14.3). The multidimensional field of the company is also a multileveled field, each level being called upon to resolve qualitatively different types of conflict.

Summary

Conflict is necessary for creativity to occur: creativity occurs when an idea arises in two conflicting or incompatible frames of reverence. A creative company will welcome conflict, it will welcome the employee who wants to upset the status quo, provided he or she wants to do so for a just reason. This conflict often shows itself as ambiguities and dilemmas. These become more complex, and have greater implication for the growth of a company, as one ascends the management hierarchy. Thus the importance of the job does not determine its level in the hierarchy. All work in a company that is directed towards producing a product as I have defined it, is important. The level is determined by the time necessary to resolve the dilemma.

If conflict is to be encouraged every endeavor must be made to ensure that poor organization has not caused it. Although we may be motivated to excel, most of us also want to belong, and be part of a productive team. By recognizing the difference between productive conflict and non-productive conflict, and by eliminating organizational conflict we will reduce the incidence of personality conflict to the minimum.

Notes

1   David A. Garvin and Michael A. Roberto, "What you don't know about making business decisions," *Harvard Business Review*, September 2001, pp. 1–8.

2   Cognitive dissonance arises when an individual must choose between atti-
    tudes and behaviors that are ambiguous.
3   See Elliott Jaques, *Requisite Organization*.

CHAPTER FIFTEEN

Non-Productive Conflict — Territory and the Manager

Before going on let me remind the reader of what I said in chapter one about the schism that lies at the heart of our being. This schism, because it lies upstream of the conscious mind, is counter-intuitive and cannot be imagined. The only way to know the truth of what I say is to know the schism directly, and often this means to be torn with profound anxiety or anguish. Human beings are not alone in suffering this wound at the heart of being; animals too are also afflicted in this way.[1] If you bear this in mind while reading the following chapter you will gain a deeper understanding of the role that territory plays in the lives of animals, and, more importantly, the role that it plays in our lives as human beings.

To begin let us first look at the part it plays in the lives of animals. By doing so we shall also be able to understand its significance in our own lives. By drawing on examples from the lives of animals I do not mean that a human being is 'nothing but' an animal, but rather that as humans we have woven into the tapestry of life units of behavior common to us and to animals.

What is territory?

"A territory," according to Robert Ardrey[2] in his book *The Territorial Imperative*, "is an area of space, whether of water or earth or air, which an animal or group of animals defend as an exclusive preserve. In most, but not all, territorial species, defense is directed against fellow members of the kind."

The need to possess territory seems to be a basic need, just as basic as the need for sexual relations. Freudian theory has persuaded us that the sexual need is the most fundamental need of humans and animals. However, studies made by ethologists leave no doubt that, for territorial animals, territory as well as sex, is fundamental. "Male animals compete for real estate, never for females. . . .The male who has not gained a territory on the stamping ground is sexually unmotivated. The female is sexually unresponsive to any male who has not succeeded in gaining territory. The doe is attracted and excited by the qualities of the property, not the qualities of the proprietor."[3] Among some species, a male that does not possess territory is impotent.

A given territory gains value as it becomes more central. Among male swans, or cobs, for example, only the most powerful cob remains for any length of time in possession of a central territory. Animals, therefore do not necessarily gain territory to ensure adequate food supply, many species of animals do not graze on their territory but seek food elsewhere. Furthermore, they are often careful to identify territorial boundaries not as an act of defiance, but to reduce the likelihood of hostility.

Obviously, then, territory has some value other than just survival value. One indication of this is that animals possessing territory have greater energy, and a challenger who wants to take possession of another's territory is almost always defeated. A male cob with a broken leg nevertheless is known to have successfully defended his territory for eight days. One could say that the possessor of territory is 'well motivated'.

Territorial combats are rarely life-and-death struggles and combatants do not often kill each other. The aim seems to be to humiliate rather than to destroy.[4] "The urge to preserve prestige and dignity is not specifically human, but lies deep in the instinctive layers of the mind which, in the higher animals, are closely related to our own." Many animals have a specific propitiating gesture and one animal will rarely attack another making this gesture. Dogs often have white fur around the throat, and this is exposed as a propitiating gesture. The fight, then, is to gain a psychological advantage and not simply physical survival. "Simple ear-lowering, horn-waggling, or other stern displays"[5] are frequently enough to discourage the challenge. What is more, when the animals are away from the territories they show no antagonism towards each other. "Should a hungry lion appear . . . the first to spot it gives a stiff legged hopping signal alerting his fellows. All retire by customary paths to wait amicably until the lion goes away."[6]

On territorial conflict and the center

Evidence that territory gives stability and that the center of the territory has a special value is given by observing sticklebacks and herring gulls. A member of both species, when fighting, will pursue its opponent into the opponent's territory. At a given point the retreating one will turn and take the offensive, pursuing the erstwhile pursuer back into his territory.

Again the time will come when the tables are turned but the distance the invader goes into the enemy's territory is gradually shortened. Eventually the two adversaries come to glower at each other across the border between their two territories. This indicates that as the one that is pursued approaches the center of its own territory so it gains in strength; as the pursuer gets further from its center it loses in strength. A dog will behave in much the same way. While close to home, that is close to its center, it can be quite vicious. As it gets further way from its center it can become increasingly timid and ready to turn and flee back to the center.

Another interesting point comes from observing the sticklebacks. When the two are about the same distance from their center they become equally matched in motivation and courage. They will then both suddenly "while goggling at each other in loathing, stand on their heads and dig holes in the sand."[7] The herring gulls, too, will reach the point of facing each other across the border: "Since they face each other not two feet apart, yet both are gripped by ferocity's storm, any observation will predict instant battle. But there will be no battle. Both gulls instead will suddenly, murderously, start pulling up grass."[8] Digging holes in the sand and ripping up grass are, for the two respective animals, nest building activities. To resolve an impossible dilemma they resort to a basic form of creativity. This is quite understandable when we remember that creativity is "a single idea in two incompatible frames of reference." The two incompatible frames of reference are the two combatants. The single idea is nest building. Such activity is called displacement activity; it can also be known as sublimation.

The importance of the boundary as well as the center

With the need for territory comes both the need to identify the boundary or periphery, and for the territory to have a center. The nearer to the center of its territory that an animal finds itself, the greater security, and therefore psychological strength, that it seems to derive. The periphery too is important. Ardrey quotes another ethologist, Frank Darling, "I would like to put forward the hypothesis that one of the important functions of territory is the provision of periphery — periphery being defined as that kind of edge where there is another bird of the same specie occupying a territory . . . . The breeding ground . . . is a place with two focal points, the nest [center] and the periphery."[9] Ardrey calls this the 'castle and border' interpretation of territory.

Territory gives a center or 'a nest', and a periphery, a border. And with this the basic schism is reconciled. This explains much territorial behavior: For example, "the possession of territory lends enhanced energy to the proprietor."[10] When we are anxious, uncertain and confused we lack motivation. In fact if we are in panic we can be quite paralyzed. The well-motivated person is one who has a single, committed intention. The 'psychological' advantage that the proprietor has over the challenger, and that which gives him enhanced energy, is just that advantage of having reconciled the two opposing points of view contained in the original viewpoint, me, through having a stable center. To have reconciled the two incompatible points of view, then, is what we call being well motivated. A small example of the value in understanding the role that territory plays in life at work is that it provides an understanding of the struggle that sometimes goes on with the question of who goes to whose office for a discussion. The one in whose office the discussion occurs will have a 'psychological ' advantage.

The challenger, by the very fact of making the challenge, is in doubt; a conflict is present within him. The advantage of the challenged is precisely the disadvantage of the challenger; let the challenged show but a moment of doubt and the advantage is lost, the territory is open for spoils. The "simple ear-lowering, horn-waggling, or other stern display" must have authority; it can only have this authority if the inherent schism or duality has been reconciled. One can observe the same phenomenon when two boxers touch gloves before the fight starts. At that moment they look each other in the eye; if one blinks he has as good as lost the fight before it begins.

The job as territory

In the corporate world we find a new kind of territory: the job. An employee's job is his territory. When we take on a job such as production manager, systems analyst, sales assistant, we have an overall idea of what that job means and that overall idea is our territory. The idea of the product of the job gives a focus, or dynamic center to that general idea. A company is an arena in which we vie for territory. A market is an arena in which companies vie for territory. Territorial behavior sheds light on behavior at work as well as the behavior of companies competing with each other for markets.

A job has both a center and a periphery. The center of a job is the product idea for the expression of which the job is established. I have called this the product of the job. On the other hand, the job has a periphery, limits; interaction is possible at the periphery with other jobs in a company. The boundary is very important, both for a job and a territory, as is the ability to mark out the boundary. The boundary of a job provides stimulation and most of a company's politics are concerned with border disputations. "There are always relationships, jobs, and policies in organization, but often they are not explicit. When they are not, there is endless possibility for the need for political maneuver; there are jealousies, misunderstandings, frustrations and conflict."[11]

A British organization theorist emphasized the importance of the boundary. He said, "the effectiveness of every inter-group relationship is determined by the extent to which groups involved have to defend themselves against uncertainty about the integrity of boundaries."[12] Task management is, according to him, essentially the definition of boundaries between task systems and the control of transactions across these boundaries. Without adequate boundary definition, frontier skirmishing is inevitable. Perhaps a major paradox of modern complex enterprises, he tells us, is that the more certainly boundaries can be located, the more easily formal communication systems can be established. "Good fences," said the poet Robert Frost, "make good neighbors."

Unless a boundary is adequately located, different people will draw it in different places and hence confusion between inside and outside will arise. In the individual this confusion can appear as anxiety and may eventually lead to a breakdown; in the enterprise this confusion appears as inefficiency, loss of morale and ultimately failure. If chaos is defined as uncertainty about boundary definition, or more colloquially, as not knowing who or what belongs where, then every transaction is potentially chaotic. "If we go further and suggest that the major characteristic of disaster is the obliteration of known boundaries, of the guides and directories which govern existence, then every transaction can be said to have built into it the elements of insipient disaster. To be continuously confused about job person boundaries, or completely unable to define and maintain boundaries, is to be mentally sick."[13]

Territorial conflict as organizational conflict

In a company in which the importance of organization is not recognized, job boundaries are badly defined, and often, in such companies, conflict will be interpreted as a conflict between personalities. Depending on the temperament of the manager in charge, this conflict will likely be dealt with either by evasion or by suppression. Few managers are willing or able to go through the delicate and trying process of sorting out the territorial claims of the protagonists.

Sometimes, unwittingly, a manager will even promote boundary conflict. He gets a new idea, calls in his subordinates, discusses it with them, and sends them away with the exhortation to "sort that out between yourselves, decide who does what, and come back to me with a plan of action." Such a manager feels that he is modern, but he has only abandoned his responsibility, rather than delegated work.

Suppose that a man A were to invite a guest to his house. A would do his best to entertain his guest well, and to have him feel relaxed and 'at home'. But suppose during the evening the guest were to let it be known that he felt he was at home! An entirely new relationship will ensue. A's problem would no longer be to get his guest to feel at home, but rather to get him out altogether.

This, in a way, is what happens sometimes when two managers get together to discuss a particular problem. At the start of the discussion one of them would feel that he 'owned' the territory, that is the subject of discussion, and would invite the other in as a guest, that is as an adviser. After a while, the guest makes it known that he in fact considers the territory his, and the conflict starts. A homeowner would probably have no difficulty in resolving his problem because he could refer to his deed of sale, and, if necessary, to the property lines or property markers. In the case of job invasion, however, one can rarely establish ownership. The deed titles, that is, the job descriptions, are generally so loosely worded that they are of little or no value in settling disputes. No attention is given to fixing adequate property markers, that is, *decision points*. Therefore, the managers would find it impossible to contest ownership at an overt level. In the absence of objective criteria, objective solutions are impossible, and subjective, that is, hidden solutions are sought. The contest is often carried on orally, and one of the ways by which some managers attempt to prove ownership of territory is to speak longer and louder about the subject in hand.

Decisions as boundaries

The boundary of a job is created by the limits of the job. Limits, used creatively become resources and so enable decisions to be made: if a manager may not spend more than $20,000 on a particular project, he can decide to spend any amount up to $20,000. The kind of decisions he makes will determine what resources should be allocated, what quality should be expected — that is, how well the product suits the needs that have been specified — and what priorities should be assigned to the task cycles involved in producing the product.

The principle decisions that a manager makes are directly related to the limits within which he works. Managers mark their territorial boundaries by initials or signatures, and these signify decisions that they have made. To define the boundaries of a job one simply determines what limits the job has, that is to say, what resources it has, and so what decisions the manager occupying the job can make. However, a boundary cannot be a boundary in isolation. Setting up a territory is both an individual act and a social act; that is, it is an act of establishing the 'self' and the 'other'. Little purpose is served by simply establishing the decision boundaries of one job. One must also establish the decision boundaries of jobs that juxtapose, and this juxtaposition will be brought about through the interaction of task cycles.

Capacity, territory authority and power

An objection that is sometimes made to the ideas that I am presenting is that just as a company is in business simply to make money for the stockholders, everyone is in a company for what they can get out of it — that no matter how well a company is organized, people will find ways to pervert it to their own ends. This was not my experience as a manager. Most of the managers that I knew had very complex reasons for working among which were greed and the lust for power, but these were by no means the over-riding reasons. Nevertheless the prevailing ethos in the corporate world is that greed is good. As human beings we are vitally affected by what others consider acceptable behavior. If we are told that greed and the lust for power are all that matter, that a company is simply in business to grab as much of these as it can, that dysfunctional relationships are the norm, then it will not be surprising to find that egoistic behavior predominates through all levels of management. For senior management in such dysfunctional companies to complain, "all workers want is more money," would be ironical to say the least.

Another reason for the 'lust for power' comes from the WCP configuration being out of equilibrium. The capacity that a person has should match his territory. The territory determines the level of work. Territory in a company is not always won, or jobs earned. People are promoted over their heads intentionally or by accident, and so territory can be conferred rather than won. When territory has been conferred and the capacity of the occupant of the job does not match the demands of the job, 'spurious power' must take the place of authority. Authority is power exercised within limits. Spurious power does not recognize limits, and therefore instead of enjoying the freedom that limits adjusted to capacity provide, the possessor of spurious power can only experience license. While freedom gives the power to act according to the circumstances, license is arbitrary.

Someone with too little territory, that is whose capacity is higher than the level of work that he has been given, will be hostile, touchy, and excitable; someone with too much territory will recoil from conflict. He will be dependent upon his host, parasite that he is; that is he will be dependent upon the one who has conferred the territory upon him. What has been given can be taken away. He would, therefore, act only in the name of his host

As long as the intention of a person is aligned with the intention of the company, he has the total power of the company and organization to back him and to provide him with authority. A person of spurious power, however, has only the intention of retaining command of his territory. This intention cannot be aligned with anything. Authority requires limits, and these limits will be provided by the job that has transformation and project cycles. The spurious power of the man whose territory is too great, who cannot cope with the transformation or project cycles, can only be exercised in unstructured situations, in situations dominated by flux. He will generate these flux situations in order to use his power; he will manage by crisis and generate non-productive conflict.

If the company has no central will with which the intention of employees can be aligned, the organization will tend to fragment, subgroups will arise, and again non-productive conflict will break out between these subgroups. The goal of discussion is to reveal the structure inherent in a situation, and this kind of discussion is an adjunct to authority. The goal of argument, on the other hand, is to tear down structure, or to so obscure the structure that a situation, for lack of a structure, becomes meaningless. Argument is the handmaiden of spurious power, and one way of generating flux.

Authority can only exist in interaction with others in authority. Power, however, can be exercised in isolation, and is its own satisfaction. The more a person is able to share with others, particularly the more he is able to share an understanding with others, the more authority he can exercise; but the more he exercises power, the more he is likely to break up understanding, reject theory, and turn discussion into argument and rebuff. In the absence of understanding, myths must arise, and these in turn will further obscure understanding.

Sticklebacks, as we saw just now, release the energy of aggression, not by attacking each other, but by adopting the entirely different behavior of nest building. In territorial combat roebucks do not attack each other but they attack the trees of the enemy. This kind of activity is called *displacement* activity. Displacement activity frequently occurs also when conflict arises between managers. Few managers relish open confrontation or argument at the eyeball-to-eyeball level. Most often in conflicts between managers the antagonists will not attack each other, but instead they may well attack the systems and procedures the other has developed. This attack can be made by undermining the confidence that others have in the other manager, in his systems, and in his ability. The effectiveness of a manager who is attacked in this way is reduced and the company as well will suffer. For lack of an overt method for satisfactorily solving territorial dispute, a whole company will suffer a kind of internal hemorrhage, and its systems can be laid to waste. And as we have seen, poor organization, which makes establishing a territory difficult for a manager to do, will increase the likelihood of territorial disputes and consequently displacement activity will likewise increase.

Ownership and territory

We can now see why addressing the relative positions of the stockholder and employees is so important. As long as stockholders are believed to 'own' the company, the problem of territory cannot be properly solved. Employees, at best, would be tenants, or sharecroppers, with no real stake in the company at all. An interesting question, and one that can always be relied upon to provide considerable stimulation to an otherwise dull meeting, is to ask people present: Who 'owns' the system under discussion? Much of the rancor that one can find in interdepartmental meetings has its origin in just that question even though no one ever overtly asks it.

Territorial conflicts between employees take place at two levels. Contrary to what one might think, at a symbolic level the conflict concerns physical territory, for example office space or parking space. At the real level the conflict concerns 'idea' territory. Territorial conflict at this level concerns itself with who owns the idea. To own an idea is to own the center of behavior space or behavior territory. Argument is often territorial conflict, and the object of the argument is to capture the idea, much in the same way that the object of battle was once to capture the enemy's capital, or the standard of the enemy, the standard being the symbol of what the enemy stands for.

The concern that we have about who owns an idea is a very real one. Many managers are familiar with the ruse of saying to a person they wish to persuade to adopt a particular idea, "that idea of yours is a very interesting one." The idea referred to, of course, is the very one that the manager wishes to have adopted.

The struggle to own and control ideas takes on a grim perspective when ideological wars are waged in order to seize or retain this ownership. The Inquisitions of the Roman Catholic Church, the concentration camps of Nazi Germany and of Stalin's Russia, the cultural revolutions of the Chinese Republic, The Cold War and the witch-hunts of the McCarthy era, the eternal conflicts in Ireland, the terrible wars in Bosnia,

Ruanda and Darfur are all forms of this ideological war — the need to control the 'minds' of human beings, which is the need to establish a territory with a particular idea as a center.

The hierarchy and the Alpha complex

The need for territory would appear to be a fact. Quoting Ardrey: "Man has an innate compulsion or instinct to gain and defend territory. It is genetic and cannot be eradicated."[14] Some writers, for example, Ashley Montague,[15] have contested this need for territory and have offered opposing evidence. However, in a study remote from concern with territory, a writer says the following, "In all times and places human beings have resisted the idea that they are nowhere for no particular reason and for no particular purpose. They have almost always managed to find somewhere to be and a reason to be there."[16] The act of finding these 'somewheres' is crucial to human life for "people seem to go to pieces when events force them to contemplate the ultimate nowhere of their lives. Then they act in ways which the majority of mankind would consider inhuman."[17]

But just as for a human being to be somewhere is important, so to be someone is equally important. The problem of being someone is closely associated with the problem of status, that is, a place in a hierarchy. The organization hierarchy is sometimes looked upon as either unnecessary or undesirable. Yet it has a firm biological basis and is not simply a human invention. We have seen when considering the work, capacity and pay equilibrium that the hierarchy is necessary because work differs in level and this difference calls for different levels of capacity. Different levels of work and capacity in turn must be matched by differences in level of pay.

The hierarchy serves the survival need of a company and has a very strong cohesive value. By serving this need the hierarchy gets its organizational and psychological value. The hierarchy is particularly emphasized in organizations that are threatened by disintegration. For example, the hierarchy is stressed in an army because an army has to face the prospect of operating in territory that it does not own and under dangerous conditions.

From the studies we have made on the center and periphery, the reason for this cohesiveness can be understood. If a territory is shared, the problem of center and periphery remains unsolved because the territory can no longer act as a neutralizing agent to the basic polarity. An alternative solution must be found, and the hierarchy provides it. As one ascends the hierarchy one approaches the center — as one descends the hierarchy, one approaches the periphery. Thus, for example, one goes 'up' through the levels of 'higher' management to 'top' management. The hierarchy achieves in the vertical dimension what territory achieves along the horizontal dimension.

The distance between levels within a hierarchy, however, must be perceptible to the members. If the distance is not perceptible, 'half-rank'[18] positions arise and again conflict will occur. The example that I gave of a manager and subordinate having WCP out of balance was an example of a 'half rank' position. The hierarchy now will no longer be able to neutralize the conflict of center and periphery. The two employees concerned will find to an increasing degree that they either avoid each other completely or will share a single job. If the latter is the case, territorial conflict will break out.

We see the same tensions generated by 'half ranks' in other areas of life. A golfer will be more likely than someone who does not play golf to be jealous of another golfer's handicap. Two people of similar status are more likely to be rivals than people of different status. At one time a gentleman would not even think of dueling with a commoner. A similar phenomenon is found among animals and is reported by Lorenz: "All social animals are `status seekers', hence there is always particularly high tension between individuals who hold immediately adjoining positions in the ranking order; conversely this tension diminishes the further apart these two animals are in rank."[19]

Human beings have a strong sense of equity or social justice and the normal human being is "committed to achieving what he judges to be his proper place in society and to taking part in social arrangements which provide the proper place for him and for everyone else. He is aware of the difference between himself and others and can judge in what respect others may be more or less competent than himself. In the absence of this sense of difference, of equity and justice, the individual is disturbed by feelings of omnipotence, or by the opposite, impotence and self-depreciation."[20]

Notes

1 For more on this see Low, *The Origin of Human Nature.*
2 Robert Ardrey, *The Territorial Imperative* (New York: Dell, 1966), p. 3.
3 *Ibid.,* p. 51.
4 *Ibid.,* p. 52.
5 *Ibid.,* p. 52.
6 *Ibid.,* p. 170.
7 *Ibid.,* p. 87.
8 *Ibid.,* p. 52.

9 *Ibid.*, p. 47.
10 *Ibid.*, p. 52.
11 W. Brown, "What is Work?" *Glacier Project Papers* (London: Heinemann, 1965), p. 70.
12 A. K. Rice, "Individual Group and Inter-Group Processes," *Human Relations*, Vol. 1, pp. 565–84. 22, No. 6, December 1969.
13 *Ibid.*
14 Ardrey, *Territorial Imperative*, p. 3.
15 Ashley Montague, *The Human Revolution* (New York: Bantam Books, 1965).
16 Paul Riesman, "The Eskimo's Discovery of Man's Place in the Universe," *Sign, Image and Symbol* (New York: Bantam Books, 1965), p. 228.
17 *Ibid.*, p. 228.
18 See Jaques, *Requisite Organization.*
19 Konrad Lorenz, *Man Meets Dog* (London: Penguin, 1964), p. 36.
20 Elliott Jaques, "Industry's Human Needs," *Management Today*, May 1970.

PART FOUR

Conflict, Creativity and Capacity

CHAPTER SIXTEEN

Commitment, Capacity and Ability

The title of this book, *Conflict and Creativity at work: the human roots of corporate life*, tells us the direction in which to look for a way to understand corporate life. I began the book by pointing out that corporate life is rooted in human nature because it is an extension of the human mind, and is isomorphic with the mind. One way that I brought home the truth of these statements was by pointing out that a one-man company, such as a cobbler, could become a multinational conglomerate. I should now like to explore this isomorphism in another, deeper way. At the same time this will give me the opportunity to expand on the definition of work that I have given and explore in much greater detail what I mean by 'the exercise of discretion'.

Our mind arises out of what I have called 'dynamic unity'. Dynamic unity when applied to achieving some result is better known as commitment. Thus the mind is not a thing, a container, but an ongoing process. At the very heart of the mind lies a conflict that arises out of two simultaneous ways of viewing or perceiving the world. I view the world simultaneously as though 'from inside' and as though 'from outside': as actor and as audience, participant and observer. Not only do I see the world in these two ways; I also see myself, 'me', in these two ways, that is from inside and from outside. 'Me' is torn in two in an impossible way. This schism or wound lies at the very heart of my experience, existence and behavior. When I act, this ambiguity is the ground from which the action arises. I am therefore faced with a constant, ongoing dilemma that has to be constantly resolved in a creative and ongoing way. Mind is not simply a process; it is an ongoing process of creativity.

A company is also the outcome of dynamic unity or commitment. The commitments of the three dimensions — stockholders employees and market — interact and create the company field. Furthermore, a company is also faced with a constant dilemma: the two horns of the dilemma being survival and self-expression. These two horns arise out of the conflicting needs of the stockholders, employees and market. This ambiguity is the ground out of which arises the work that goes on in a company, and so the company too is an ongoing creative process.

Traditionally companies were divided into what was called 'line' departments and 'staff departments'. Although the difference between these two kinds of departments was intuitively recognized, the real difference was rarely understood because of the univalent manner of understanding a company. If the function of the company was looked upon as making as much money as possible for the stockholder, and as the product was the way that that money could be gotten hold of, those departments that produced the product were the important ones; the rest of the company simply passed the tools when they were wanted, and advised and assisted the line departments in the process of using those tools. Line departments did the real work; staff departments were a necessary evil.

If, on the contrary, a company is looked at from a multivalent point of view then 'staff departments' are those departments concerned with the survival aspect of the company and 'line departments' are concerned with the expressive aspect of the company. They are all concerned with producing the main product.

Dynamic unity and commitment

Commitment is the dynamo of a company. The definition of work would in fact be better expressed as, 'work is *commitment* — through the exercises of discretion within limits — to produce a product', because in order to do work and produce a product commitment is essential. Moreover commitment is not possible without a corresponding need. In the present chapter I shall write about commitment and its connection to need. In the next chapter I shall write about 'discretion'.

Each is an individual, but we are not only one, we are a dynamic, intentional and purposeful one. We have an urge to do, to commit ourselves. One of the perennial problems in management is how to 'motivate' employees. Buried in 'wanting to motivate employees' is the false assumption that human beings normally want to be at rest, and only get into action because of some outer stimulation, some promise of reward or threat of punishment. To disprove this patently false notion one only has to decide to sit and do nothing and then see for how long one is able to do so. Will, intention, commitment, dedication, devotion, resolve, as well as motivation, all these are implied in the term 'dynamic unity', the origin of all our activity and the very basis of life. The problem, therefore, is not how to motivate people so much as how to remove obstructions to their commitment.

The drive to belong

We express dynamic unity in our lives in the *drive to be unique*, which underlies our ambition, competitiveness, the need to win, excel and to get ahead. With all that has been said about ambiguity we should not be surprised to learn that the drive to be unique is accompanied by a contradictory drive, which is also the expression of dynamic unity. This is *the drive to belong*. Karen Horney,[1] a psychologist of the thirties and forties, said that human beings have the drive to belong as well as the need for power, prestige and possessions. These latter three are the outcome of the drive to be unique, but the drive to belong is as strong as the drive to be unique. Because of it we have the need for family, friends and neighbors. We also enjoy being members of a group, members of a sports team or members of a project team. Without this drive a tribe, country or civilization would be impossible. Without it a company too would be impossible. Modern Western society has emphasized and encouraged our competitive nature to the detriment of our drive to belong, and much of the feeling of alienation, loneliness and isolation that is so widespread occurs because the drive to belong is denied satisfaction.

Because these two drives — to be unique and to belong — are contradictory and going in opposite directions, they create their own kind of tension, and various strategies have evolved to reduce this tension. Fashions, titles, uniforms, medals, certificates, are all ways by which we can be distinctive and stand out from the group, while at the same time belong to the group.

On different levels of commitment, capacity and ability

The idea that 'all men are born equal' is basic to our political institutions, but at the same time, our economic institutions are based upon free enterprise, and in them we are very unequal. The philosophical bases of the Western economic institutions are still the laissez-faire philosophies of Adam Smith and other like-thinking social philosophers of the nineteenth century, even though governments have modified the extent to which the enterprise is free. Laissez-faire, in theory, allows people to compete freely in order that the fittest might survive, and it assumes that the fittest will, in the process, benefit society by providing not only for themselves, but for others as well. Laissez-faire and the notion that all men are born equal are two basic premises of Western democracies — and they are contradictory.

For a long time people believed that if someone were to work hard enough, he or she would be bound to succeed. This myth was based upon the myth of the equality of human beings. The French boasted that in Napoleon's army every soldier carried a field marshal's baton in his haversack. But it is obvious that no matter how hard some people may work, however much education they receive, they will never rise very high in the management hierarchy. On the other hand, others are able to rise through the management levels apparently without a great deal of effort. So although human equality may be a fact, human inequality is also a fact, and because of inequality one person may rise to the head of a company while another finds a supervisory level too difficult. It might be said that this is simply because one has more friends in high places, more education, the right sort of experience, or more luck than another. All of these may be contributing factors, but the potential for operating at higher levels in the organizational hierarchy arises mainly out of *the capacity and ability to do work and the willingness to commit that capacity and ability within a particular framework.* Each of these three primary dimensions — commitment, capacity and ability — is in itself a complex structure. We shall find that we all have them in unequal measure.

I started this chapter by saying that I would show another way in which the human being and the company that he creates are isomorphic. The nine dimensional structure of a company — three power holders, three integrating functions and three process functions — will correspond to a nine dimensional structure of commitment, capacity, and ability.

Commitment and need

Needs, desires, wants, as I have said, are the precursors of commitment. We must need something before being willing to commit ourselves to attaining it. The interaction of needs and different levels of needs gives rise to the richness of the personality and to the infinite variety of ways in which the commitment of human beings is focused. Commitment modified by needs, brings about different kinds of action and interaction. For example, uniqueness is sought after at all levels: at the *level of truth* (third level) we seek it by coming up with new ideas and claiming them as our own; at the *level of possession* (second level) we seek uniqueness through the exclusiveness of possession; at the *physical level* (first level) we seek it through the idiosyncrasies of behavior.

In the sixties Abraham Maslow[2] suggested that we have a hierarchy of needs, and his suggestion was widely accepted. The needs in his hierarchy started at physical needs and ascended through the need for security and safety, community, status and recognition, and the need for self-actualization. About the same time, Robert Ardrey in his studies suggested a triad of needs: the need for security, the need for stimulation, and the need for identity.

I am suggesting that we are physical, social, and spiritual beings, and have needs that correspond to each of these levels. At the first, physical level, we need activity, comfort, and sustenance. At the second, social level, we need power, prestige, and possessions. At the third, spiritual level, we need justice, beauty, and truth. Finally two conflicting overall drives are at work in us: the drive to be unique and the need for unity and harmony that I have called the drive to belong.

Commitment, focused by need, provides the precipitating point, the center of gravity around which all experience is structured. The name given to the center of gravity is 'I', and 'I' gives a sense of unique identity. A sense of identity allows us to play the role of parent, spouse, employee, friend, and so on. As a parent I find my identity as a father; as a spouse, it is as a husband; as an employee, it is as salesperson or lawyer, bus driver or company president. When commitment is congruent — that is, when needs, modified by the various roles that we play, mutually

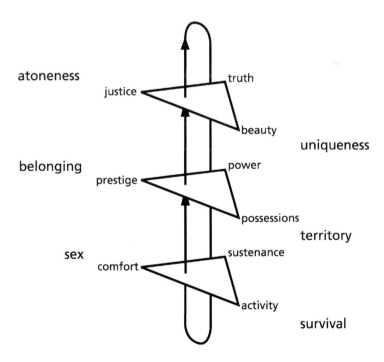

Figure 16.1 Hierarchy of needs

support each other — then we feel at one, solid in our commitment, settled and secure. The way we commit ourselves, and what we commit ourselves to, gives our lives degrees of richness and harmony. The more unified the basic commitment, the greater the inner coherence and the happier we feel.

Figure 16.1 sets out what I have said about needs in the form of a diagram. The arrows stand for dynamic unity. The fact that the arrows go in two directions illustrates the two conflicting ways of viewing the world. In going up towards oneness or wholeness, dynamic unity acts as an integrating force. At the physical level this is expressed in sexual activity; at the social level it is expressed as belonging; at the spiritual level it is expressed as what I call at-one-ment. This is the level that includes peace, love, and harmony. In going down from uniqueness as a differentiating, expressive force, at the spiritual level dynamic unity is expressed as the need to be a unique person, 'I'; at the social level it is expressed as the need for territory, while at the physical level the need it is expressed as the need to survive as an autonomous unit.

As I have already pointed out, each level has its own set of needs: at the physical level are the needs for comfort, sustenance and activity; at the social level are the needs for power, prestige and possessions; at the spiritual are the needs for the good the true and the beautiful.

Dynamic unity and creativity

The kind and degree of commitment that we give changes constantly as circumstances change; it changes both in direction (from survival to self-expression) and in level, as well as in type. In addition, we are torn by a basic dilemma and so are constantly confronted by dilemmas in life experience and at work. Many of these simply cannot be resolved, and so we bury the unresolved horn, which even so pushes for satisfaction. At each moment we can commit but a fraction of ourselves. All that is not committed, and all the needs that are thereby not satisfied remain in the background as audience, critics, or perhaps even as enemies. All of which inflicts upon us the burden that comes from the feeling of some-thing seeming to have been missed, of some unfulfilled promise. We lose the feeling of being at one, happiness is replaced by anxiety and tensions, and our security gives way to insecurity and vulnerability.

Creativity, which is our over-riding need, is dynamic unity in action. Work therefore should allow us to satisfy simultaneously many needs at different levels. The money earned buys the various things we need. The work environment gives an opportunity to belong, to exercise power through authority or through having more knowledge. It affords status symbols, prestige, and territory. At a higher level we can promote justice and fair play and increase our understanding. Thus through the job we do in a well organized company we can attain integration, achieve self-confidence, and expand our activities and experiences — and perhaps even grow.

Notes

1   Karen Horney, *The Neurotic Personality of Our Time* (New York: Norton, 1937).

2   Abraham Maslow, *Towards a Psychology of Being* (New York: Van Nostrand, 1962).

CHAPTER SEVENTEEN

On Capacity and Ability

'Work is commitment — through *the exercise of discretion* within limits — to produce a product', and we exercise discretion through our capacity and ability to do the work required. Capacity has three dimensions: level of *perception*, of *stress tolerance*, and of *communication*; ability also has three dimensions: level of *intelligence* and *skill*, of *education* and *training*, and of *'fit-in-ability'*. The isomorphism of a company and the mind is clearly shown when we examine the meaning of the words 'capacity' and 'ability'. Capacity corresponds to the structural dimension of a company, while ability corresponds to the process dimension. Commitment could be looked upon as a kind of power with capacity and ability being the conduit through which it flows. If the conduit is too narrow the power will become dammed, if it is too wide the power will lose its effectiveness. Capacity corresponds to the diameter of the conduit; ability is the conduit itself.

Capacity

Some people have great capacity but little ability. They are often ambitious without the means to satisfy their ambition. They are often impractical, having the vision without the ability to make that vision into a workable program. They are often impatient, wanting immediate recognition and satisfaction. All of this makes them tend to take shortcuts to satisfaction and they may end up as gamblers, or even criminals.

On the other hand, some can have great ability and little capacity. They are likely to be the perfect bureaucrats, knowing and adhering closely to all the rules and regulations. Because they are often very efficient they are likely to be promoted over their level of capacity. They are likely to be very logical and unwilling to take a risk.

Level of perception

The most important concern in business is not coming up with the right solution, but coming up with the right problem. If one comes up with the wrong solution to the right problem, probably not too much damage is done, but if one comes up with the right answer to the wrong problem, one can ruin a company. "In so far as top managers ask the wrong questions and muster poor intelligence, wrong decisions will be more efficiently arrived at and poor judgment, buttressed by quantitative data, will be made more effective."[1]

Many companies have gone bankrupt because, with competence and expertise, they have been seeking to solve the wrong problems. A dozen computers working twenty-four hours a day on the wrong problem will simply turn out a mess. The French Maginot Line of 1939 was a perfect answer, but the question that the French posed was wrong. They were seeking to solve the problem of how to fight trench warfare with none of the inconvenience of trench warfare. The real problem was one of how to fight a mobile war, and so their reliance on the Maginot Line was a disaster.

If you know the problem, you know where to look for the answer, but what tells you where to look for the problem? I have made the distinction between the urgent and the important. Finding solutions is normally urgent; finding problems is important. I also said when the important becomes urgent one encounters a crisis. One must see problems before they arrive. The greater the problem the more time will be necessary to deal with it, and so the further into the future one must be able to look. One aspect of the level of perception is the distance one can see into the future. It is like the higher you go up a hill the further you can see.

Much of management literature today is devoted to leadership: what are the qualities of a good leader, how one can be a good leader, what to avoid as a good leader. The minimum requirement for a good leader is to have a vision, an idea that calls for action. The best ideas will not be found in seeking answers, but in commitment to areas of unexplored possibilities. These often present themselves as what 'cannot be done', as 'too difficult to tackle', as 'the impossible'. We do not find these unexplored possibilities by thinking, but through being willing to be open and so able to see beyond the obstacles. The kind of openness that I refer to cannot be attained in a poorly organized company in which conflict is frowned upon, and in which territorial disputes are generated through inadequate job definition and vague boundaries. Openness includes being open to dilemma, ambiguity, conflicting ideas and possibilities.

The perception of ideas is best termed a 'cosmic-organic' process.

Ideas are not ours to own, but simply ours to perceive and express. Simultaneous discoveries illustrate what I mean; for example, the discovery of calculus by both Newton and Leibniz and the theory of evolution by Darwin and Wallace. The notion of the seer as a semi-divine being, and the prevalence of magic and superstition in primitive cultures, all arise out of the recognition that ideas are conceived in the cosmos but perceived by the organism.

Life does not simply present us with problems but with multifaceted dilemmas each aspect of which demands a response. Level of perception therefore means level of openness to ambiguity and the ability to use the mind in non-logical ways. The fact that something has always been done in a particular way might be the very reason for no longer doing it in that way.

Creative thinking and logical thinking are quite different. The first calls for the perception (of ideas) and the second the intellectual process of analytical thought. Such a distinction is not new and many authors and researchers of mental processes have noted these two different ways of 'thinking'. Oswald Spengler, for example, contrasts them when he states: "The destiny idea demands life experience and not scientific experience; the power of seeing and not that of calculating, depth and not intellect."[2] Perception ends in action; intellect in a logical formulation. Perception therefore concerns itself with a totality, a whole, while the intellect concerns itself with parts. Perception concerns itself with the idea, the intellect with the fact that expresses that idea. Perception is immediate, timeless; intellect is in time, it passes through stages.

The distinction between perception and analytical thinking is at the root of some critical re-evaluation that was given to the MBA program. It has been found in the past, for example, that the median salaries of graduates of the Harvard Business School plateau approximately fifteen years after the graduate enters business and, on the average, do not increase significantly thereafter. Thus, the growth of most business graduates seemed to level off just at the time when people who are destined for top management typically show their greatest rate of advancement. This suggests that people "who get to the top in management have developed skills that are not taught in formal management education programs and may be difficult for highly educated men to learn on the job."[3] But it further suggests that capacity and ability are quite different.

So disenchanted was Peter Drucker with management training that he has suggested that one of the qualifications for obtaining a management position be that the contender not have a university degree.[4] In a similar way George Bernard Shaw said that the advantage of going to university is knowing that one would have missed nothing by not going. Another writer says that problem finding is more important than problem solving and involves cognitive processes that are very different and much more complex. "While the analytical skills needed for problem solving are important, more crucial to managerial success are the perceptual skills needed to identify problems long before evidence of them can be found by even the most advanced management system. Since these perceptual skills are extremely difficult to develop in the classroom, they are now largely left to be developed on the job."[5]

Whereas level of perception is the first dimension of capacity, level of intelligence (skill) is the first dimension of ability.

The marketing dimension is that dimension which is concerned with perceiving the market's needs that can be satisfied by the product. In other words it sets the problem that the product has to solve. The level of perception in an individual is therefore the counterpart of the Marketing function within a company, while the level of intellectual skill or intelligence is the counterpart of the Product-Development function.

Level of stress tolerance

To do work one must first perceive the dilemma. I have used the word 'dilemma' to cover what might also be called a dissonant field. I have said that managers are faced with quadrilemmas as well as dilemmas, and they are often faced with a number of dilemmas and quadrilemmas at the same time and many of these may well be nested in other dilemmas and quadrilemmas. As I do not want to complicate the terminology I will simply use the word 'dilemma'. The higher the level of the dilemma, the longer the time span required to resolve it. To express fully an idea one must not only perceive it, but one must also retain the idea within the dissonant field of stress generated by the dilemma for the time it takes to express the idea. The tension is generated by the horns of a dilemma, which demand equal and simultaneous attention.

Hans Selye, who pioneered research into stress, suggested that we have an energy that enables us to cope with stress. The energy was hypothetical as far as he was concerned, and he confessed that he did not know what this energy might be. "It is as though we have hidden resources of adaptability, or adaptation energy, in ourselves throughout the body . . . Only when all our adaptability is used up will irreversible, general exhaustion and death set in . . . The term 'adaptation energy' has been coined for that which is consumed during continued adaptive work, to indicate that it is something different from the caloric energy received from food . . . We still have no precise concept of what this energy might be."[6]

'Adaptation energy' is dynamic unity. People, who are committed to what they are doing, who feel their lives have a purpose, have a high energy level and so are less prone to suffer from the ill effects of stress. Selye would no doubt have agreed that creativity and work are our ultimate needs. He saw each individual as different, having a different tolerance and a different level at which he or she can create and work. "In order to express fully, you must first find your optimum stress, and then use your adaptation energy at a rate and in a direction adjusted to the innate structure of your mind and body."[7]

Stress tolerance enables one to stay with the whole situation in all its chaotic randomness. "The manager cannot manage well unless he in some sense manages all. Specifically he must have some idea of what the whole relevant world is like, to be able to justify that which he manages, if managed correctly."[8] For example, a salary administration system combines the elements: job descriptions, job levels, pay scales, budgets, salary surveys, as well as employees expectations, among other elements. When setting up a salary admin system one must find out how to define these elements, how to combine them into a system, and then how to relate the system to the management that must operate it and to the employees affected by it. Whoever develops the system must also have an idea of what other systems are being introduced at the same time and so the amount of time that others can give to introducing his system.

All this must be carried on within the limits of the full dilemma that I outlined in chapter seven, and whoever is developing the system will feel stressed. Stress is reduced either by surrendering the product idea (failing), or by expressing it (succeeding). Some stress is necessary for the person to feel challenged, but the situation becomes unbearable to the extent that stress reaches and passes a given threshold. The level of the threshold is a function of what I am calling stress tolerance. The capacity to bear stress, to tolerate incompleteness, to carry the burden of waste and risk, and to face and resolve the dilemmas inherent in management is stress tolerance. Managers must be those "who are comfortable in the presence of risk, who have a high tolerance for ambiguity and uncertainty."[9]

If perception is related to the Marketing function, stress tolerance has its counterpart in a company organization and in the competence of the people in the organization. A well-organized company with competent personnel has a high stress tolerance. Thus stress tolerance can be related to the Human Resources function of a company.

Level of communication or empathy

The power to do work includes the power to perceive an idea, to hold that idea in the face of dilemmas, and to work out the implications of that idea. But it also includes sensitivity to the environment. Such sensitivity implies an interaction between oneself and others, and could also be called *empathy* or even *compassion*. It is expressed through communication. The level of communication is therefore the third dimension of capacity.

Some people can perceive an idea, and can sustain the tension of the dilemma, but are rigid and inflexible in their behavior. They can take all sorts of knocks, but nothing changes them — they seem to be unable to mature. A mature person can change his idea or the way that he is expressing that idea according to feedback that he gets from his environment. He can do so without abandoning the work he is engaged in. Such responsiveness is related to empathy, which in turn is the foundation of communication. We can interact without empathy, but without it we cannot communicate.

A sensitive person is empathetic, recognizing the other as another person, and not as simply a role. We lack this sensitivity when seeing a 'sales assistant', 'a teller', a 'policeman', and not people. In the same way we often see an 'employee', or a 'manager', and forget the human being in the role. When we do so we interact, we do not communicate; we interact with others in the same way we interact with objects.

Within a company meaningful communication — as distinct from conversation —is often about decisions. Conversations are often about opinions. A decision differs from an opinion in that a decision has the means by which it can be made effective. To make a decision is an action. Command of the necessary financial and other resources enables a decision to become an effective action within an organization. Budgets or, better still, resource feed flow systems are therefore the primary means by which decision making, and therefore effective communication within an organization, is made possible. Finance could be considered to be the 'carrier wave' of communication within a company.

Therefore the level of communication within a company is a function of the budget or resource feed flow system within that company. Communication, in the sense described above in regard to an individual, corresponds to the Treasury and Budgeting functions within a company.

Ability

In the same way that the three dimensions of capacity correspond to the three dimensions of organization as structure, so the abilities of a person correspond to the organization as process. Ability has three dimensions: skill, education, and compatibility. In considering these three we shall see that skill corresponds to the product development dimension, education and experience to product processing, and compatibility to the sales/service dimension.

Level of skill

Skill is the first requirement necessary for expressing an idea. Skill may be mental or physical. In the technical, non-managerial aspects of work, motor skills, such as typing, using a computer, and with blue collar workers, operating a machine and using tools of some sort, are often necessary and a wide diversity, as well as level, of these skills exists. In the managerial aspect of work, intelligence or mental skills are necessary. A number of tests have been designed to determine the level of a person's intelligence. These normally test the ability to manipulate numbers, to understand verbal expressions or words, and to reason deductively and analogically.

Level of experience

Education, training and experience together are the second dimension of ability; in the sphere of business, education and training are, or at least should be, condensed and systematized experience. Intelligence enables a person to conceptualize and quantify plans, but training and experience provide the equipment and structures necessary to carry these plans into action. Without this equipment the plans may well be abortive.

Compatibility or fitinablity

People frequently fail to get a job simply because they do not fit in. Religion, nationality, size, weight, sex, color and other factors, play a part even though the law prohibits discrimination on these grounds.

Intelligence and skill correspond to the Product Development function, education and training to the Product Processing and fit-in-ability to the Product Linking function.

The variability of capacity and ability

The three capacity dimensions vary independently of each other. Someone may have very high perception, very low stress tolerance, and average empathy with others. Or alternatively, he might have very low perception, very low stress tolerance, and high empathy with others. Generally speaking, the original thinker will have a high level of perception, the generalist will have a high level of stress tolerance, and the good salesperson will have a high level of empathy.

Someone with limited capacity but high ability is like a company that has too much equipment or too many systems, and must spend a disproportionate amount of time maintaining the systems and servicing the equipment. This kind of person, who passes exams through sheer commitment but lacks the capacity to understand what they are learning, makes Drucker and Shaw skeptical of the value of education. Alternatively, someone with too much capacity and too little ability is like a company that has grown too fast: it has considerable potential in the market, its employees are well motivated, and it has very good credit, but its systems are inadequate, its manufacturing systems and machinery are poor, and its ability to sell and service is lacking. Such a company would first need to set its house in order by establishing its process dimensions. In the same way this person should get more education.

The company's systems, its standard practices and procedures, are

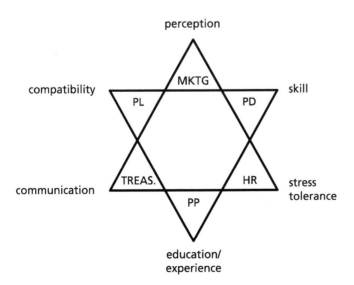

Figure 17.1 Capacity and ability related to a company

similar to an individual's education. A company with a good set of systems that are well indexed and readily accessible is like a well-educated person. On the other hand, a company with a poor set of systems is like a badly educated person. A company with a good set of systems that are poorly indexed is something like a person who has an education but a poor memory and is therefore unable to make use of the education he or she has received. The skill that a company has could be related to the tools and machinery, equipment, and instruments that are available to the people.

Notes

1 Chris Argyris, "How Tomorrow's Executives Will Make Decisions," *Think*, November–December 1967, p.18.

2 Oswald Spengler, *The Decline of the West* (London: George Allen and Unwin, 1932), p. 202.

3 J. S. Livingston, "Myth of the Well-Educated Manager," *Harvard Business Review*, January–February 1971, pp. 79–89.

4 Peter Drucker, *Our Top-Heavy Corporations*, interview in Dun's Review, April 1971, pp. 38–41.

5 Livingston, "Myth of the Well-Educated Manager," p. 80.

6 Hans Selye, *The Stress of Life* (New York: McGraw-Hill, 1956), p. 66.

7 *Ibid.*, p. 67.

8 C. W. Churchman, *Challenge to Reason* (New York: McGraw-Hill, 1968).

9 "The New Management Finally Takes Over," *Business Week*, August 1969.

PART FIVE

Ownership and Ethics

CHAPTER EIGHTEEN

A Question of Ownership

People normally see a company as *univalent*: a linear descent from the board of directors through the managers and employees to the customer. The univalent view has as its corollary the belief that a company is 'simply in business to make a profit', a belief that is one of the most fundamental in the credo underlying the free enterprise system. It needs to be examined carefully. Profit making for the stockholder and free enterprise are often seen to be either synonymous, or at least Siamese twins. As these are further coupled with democracy it would seem only the foolhardy would want to question this basic belief. Yet even so, the despoliation of the atmosphere and environment, as well as the corporate scandals of the eighties and nineties must make even the strongest devotee wonder whether he has misplaced his faith, and whether the time has come for a fresh look at what is really going on. The vexed question, "Who owns a corporation?" is a way into seeing what really is going on.

Entrepreneurial management and professional management

Let us distinguish between the entrepreneurial and the professional company. The failure to make such a distinction is at the root of much misunderstanding. The example that I gave of the cobbler is an example of an entrepreneurial company. The cobbler was the owner of his company. He stood to win or lose according to the fortunes of the company. His friends, the investors, also were part owners: it was with their money that rent was paid, machinery and raw materials were bought. They stood to lose their entire investment if the cobbler had made a bad assessment of the market or of his ability to satisfy it.

The cobbler's idea is the center of gravity of the company. Before he came on the scene the business did not exist. Moreover, the investors may have invested in his idea because they liked him, but they also invested because they knew that as his business grew so their share in the company would grow as well. As he made a profit so they expected he would share some of it with them. They also expected to have some control over any major decisions he would make that would affect the security of their investment. However, it was the cobbler who recruited or employed them. He asked them if they would join in his enterprise.

Profit for the cobbler was what remained after he had paid his expenses, and these expenses would have included paying his employees *as well as* his investors, and also returning some of the money earned back into the company for future growth and contingencies. His 'salary' and his 'profit' would have been indistinguishable.

But earning money was only part of his concern. He also wanted a livelihood, an outlet for his creativity, and an interesting and challenging way to live. The company gave an outlet for his creativity at various levels, gave him a feeling of autonomy and it also gave him the opportunity to provide a service to the community. The company was an extension of his personality.

A publicly traded professional company is different. The major stock-holders, represented by the Board of Directors (in theory at least), employ the president and determine his salary and his other financial rewards. He comes into an existing company and so has to adapt to the prevailing idea of the company. He has therefore an entirely different relation to the company than had the entrepreneur who started it. The same is true of the investors. When a company goes public, the stockholders have a different and much diminished relation to the company when compared to the original stockholders. They not only have a limited liability, they also have a limited interest, and limited control.

Stockholders that invest through the stock exchange are no longer investors in companies but speculators in shares. The original investor sought return on investment and growth, the public investors also look for these, but they also want *liquidity*. Before a company goes public, the stockholder's investment is fixed, and to liquidate it is difficult, if not impossible, except by selling the company or by the company failing. Once the shares are sold on the open market the situation is quite different: the stockholder can liquidate the shares, although sometimes at a price. One buys shares in the hope that their price will rise. This rise may be due to the management of the company, but it may also be due, and very often is, to a general fluctuation of the market. For example, interest rates change and the market responds accordingly.

The need for liquidity creates a hiatus, a gap, between the stockholder and the company, a gap that did not exist before the shares were sold on the open market. The gap changes the relation of stockholder and company in a qualitative way. A gambler at a casino table, when he buys the chips with which he plays does not invest in the casino. The chips represent a reserve of capital that fluctuates in value according to the fluctuations of chance. The casino, furthermore, is not there to make a profit for the gambler and, ultimately, the other gamblers pay the gambler when he wins. Of course the analogy breaks down in many ways, but the essential, the relation that the gambler has to the casino, and the relation a stockholder has to the stock exchange, is very similar. Most often I do not invest in a company; I invest in a stack of chips (shares), which fluctuate in value, mainly through the influence of forces out of the control of the company in which I have invested. I do not therefore own part of a company; I own the chips, that is, shares of a company. This becomes very obvious when, as is the case with so many people, I invest through a mutual fund, or through the money I have paid into a pension fund and which the pension manager invests on my behalf. The portfolio of most mutual funds is very wide and the number of companies invested in is equally large. I need liquidity in order to gamble, and by acquiring liquidity I relinquish any real control, and therefore any claim to ownership of the company.

Marjorie Kelly, in her book *The Divine Right of Capital*, quoted from a book called *The Modern Company and Private Property*, written in 1954 by Adolf Berle, at one time the Assistant Secretary of State. She said that the book was famous for noting the separation of ownership and control in the modern corporation. The author was the first to observe that company owners had dropped their management function. By the time of its 1967 revision, Berle was observing that stockholders had dropped yet another function: that of providing capital. He wrote:

"Stock markets are no longer places of 'investment' . . . .. [They are] only psychologically connected with the capital gathering and capital application system on which productive industry and enterprise actually depend . . . . The purchaser of stock does not contribute savings to an enterprise . . . he merely estimates the chance of the corporation's shares increasing in value. The contribution his purchase makes to anyone other than himself is the maintenance of liquidity for other stockholders who may wish to convert their holdings into cash."[1]

As Kelly points out, the dollars that an investor pays for the shares do not go to corporations but to other speculators. "Among the Dow Jones Industrials only a handful have sold any common stock in thirty years. According to figures from the Federal Reserve in recent years only one in a hundred dollars trading on the public markets has been reaching corporations. Those who found the company do take a risk based on company activity. Those who buy sixth and seventh hand take a gambler's risk."[2]

Who owns the company?

Most people believe that stockholders own the company. But do they in fact do so? Do they own the company or do they own shares in a company? This is an important distinction because on the answer that is given rests the understanding that we have of a company. To own implies to be able to control and to be responsible for. 'Ownership-responsibility-control' are interdependent. Do stockholders control a company; are they responsible for what it does? It might be said in so far as the stockholders elect the board of directors, and the board of directors selects the president, that the stockholder indeed is in control. But is this the best way to account for the facts? For example, J. K. Galbraith said some time ago that the annual meeting of the large business company "is perhaps a most elaborate exercise in popular illusion because with great unction and little plausibility, corporate ceremony seeks to give the stockholder an impression of power. When the entrepreneur owned the company he shared ownership with a few powerful stockholders, who ran the company with him. There was comparatively little pomp and ceremony. But as the stockholder gets less power, more ceremony is required."[3]

The decline of power, moreover, is not confined simply to the stockholder; it has extended to the board of directors. Even the board, which once sat at the right hand of the source of all economic power, must change its role. Its control is a control in theory rather than in practice and has been for some time. Some time ago in 1971 *Business Week* said, "One of the totems of business is the board of directors. That august body, once synonymous with power, prestige, and probity, is now under attack. Its critics call it an ornamental anachronism and charge that board members no longer protect the interests of stockholders."[4] It seems that boards merely rubber stamp what managers have already decided, and can protect the interests of stockholders only when those interests coincide with those of the managers.

In 2003 Marjorie Kelly says much the same, "Corporate governance is a field where stockholders reign supreme, because they are considered owners rather than mere investors. It's a curious field. In poring over corporate governance materials recently, I've come away with the feeling that, as author Gertrude Stein once put it, 'There's no there there:' In theory, boards of directors are elected by stockholders, but in reality they're handpicked by the CEO and the previous board, and rubber-stamped by stockholders. Again in theory, boards govern in stockholders' interests, but mostly they choose a chief executive officer, who does the rest. Once in a while they vote on a takeover or merger offer. That's pretty much it."[5]

One company president, irritated that his directors did not give him total control, said: "I didn't get to be president by soliciting a lot of opinions, then getting a consensus of everybody around, and going along with the majority — and that's one of the reasons our board has never really shaped up."[6] A company director is reported to have said: "The reason I don't get involved as an outside board member is that I don't have time to get the facts, and I prefer not to look stupid. Silence is a marvelous cover."[7] It would further seem that "in most large and medium-sized companies where the president and board members own only a few shares of stock, the president determines what boards will do. In most cases this means that the board is relegated to performing functions that are substantially diluted from the classical jobs of policymakers and guardians of the stockholders' interests."[8]

Who owns what?

If stockholders say that they own the company what do they claim to own? Again the question arises, "What is a company?" We have already seen that the company is not the building that houses it, or the equipment, appliances and machinery that are used by the employees. In any case, if any one owns these it would be the employees who use them. Does not a manager say, "Come to *my* office and let's discuss that?" Does not the computer technician talk about "*my* computer"? or the salesman talks about "*my* car," even though the company has bought all three?

I defined a company as a holonic, multidimensional field of commitment capable of growth, expansion, and self-regulation, having the contradictory drives to survive and to fulfill its mission, with a product as its dynamic center. The field is obviously not a physical field, but it is not a psychological field either. It is a denizen of Popper's third world. So how can it be owned? I can own a car, a house, a yacht, I can even own intellectual property in the form of a copyright, but how can one own a field of commitment, or a network of ideas? The cobbler owned the materials, machinery, possibly he also owned the factory in which these were housed. Of course he shared ownership with others, but the point is what he and they owned jointly was something concrete. The change from the cobbler's company to a modern company, whose shares are sold on the open market, requires a quantum leap from a private company that can be owned and a public company that cannot.

Although the meaning of ownership has changed in that it has become a much more complex notion than 'this is mine and that is yours', the attitudes and beliefs that it once bred remain unchanged. To change these attitudes would need a prodigious exercise of thought and will, and to leave well enough alone is easier and more comfortable — at least on the surface. But, paradoxically, to leave well enough alone means considerable rationalization, frustration, and even chaos. It would not be so bad if those who performed the magic of turning Cinderella stockholders into queens for a day were not taken in by their own magic; but they are.

Management/employee dichotomy

An example of the kind of chaotic thinking and activity that confusion of ownership can cause is the management/employee dichotomy, one of the most pervasive dichotomies that arises out of the univalent view of a corporation. A great deal of confusion has been created by this dichotomy because it naturally implies that managers are not employees; an implication that is reinforced when managers discuss employees: "All that employees really want is as much money for as little work as they can get." "A company is not there for the good of its employees." And so on. When a manager says this, he is talking about them — the employees — not himself.

But the question naturally arises: if the manager is not an employee, what is he? The stockholder-owner illusion becomes useful in providing an answer, which is why many managers support the notion 'we-are-in-business-for-the-stockholder'. Given the polarity owner/employees, managers gravitate toward the mythical 'owners' as their source of power. Many, particularly senior managers, feel offended if they are reminded that they too are employees, and so are not different in kind from the rank and file. Allegiance to a mythical source in turn reinforces the belief in the univalent view of organization. Power is vested at the top and percolates uni-dimensionally through the organization. Great emphasis is then put on the organization chart with the board of directors, and sometimes even the stockholders, at the top. Without that powerhouse at the top, a manager would only have his own resources on which to rely for his power in a company.

A kind of confusion — no, irony would be the better word — sometimes shows up because of the management-employee dichotomy. The company that I worked for suffered a fairly long strike. The main grievance was pay. The union felt that the blue-collar workers were not being paid enough. In order to keep the company going the supervisors and managers had to fill the jobs vacated by the blue collar workers on strike, and do as much of the work as possible. Eventually, the company agreed to the union's demands.

The irony is the following. The union gained something like a ten percent increase. (This was during the time of inflation.) Now, the first line supervisors' pay grade started at ten percent above the highest blue-collar worker. After the pay increase was given to the blue-collar workers, many supervisors were being paid at the same rate as the blue-collar workers, or just slightly above. The lack of a pay differential obviously could not continue and so the company increased the pay grades, and the pay, for the supervisors. But these pay grades were a fixed percentage lower than the pay grades for first line managers. The increase for the supervisors eroded the differential, which was obviously not acceptable. So the management pay grades (and pay) were automatically increased by ten percent and so the increase percolated up the hierarchy. The supervisors, and many managers, did their best to end the strike by reducing the impact that it had on the customers, yet the outcome of the strike was to give the supervisors and managers the very increase that they were trying to deny to the blue-collar workers.

The philosophy of the managers who bargained with the union representatives was to give as little as possible to the employees so that more profit could be given to the stockholders. The managers therefore bargained against their own interest. The theory behind the company negotiations was that the company should pay an increase equivalent to the increased cost of living over the previous year plus a 'part of the pie'. The pie was, theoretically, the increase in the fortunes of the company, but practically the blue collars' part of the pie was as little as possible.

The union was bargaining on a much more solid base. It was asking for as much of an increase as it and other unions had obtained from other companies in recent contract negotiations with them. Whether it did so consciously or intuitively I do not know. But they were undoubtedly arguing for the employees which is something that the managers should have been doing, but which they could not do because the 'company is in business to make a profit'. The real bargaining should have been between the Finance, Human Resources and Marketing functions to share out the 'pie' equitably between the three power groups.

On the one hand, managers were bargaining on behalf of the stock-holder, ostensibly to increase the money that could be paid out to them; on the other hand, they were obviously bargaining for themselves. I was one of the managers, and although I worked to keep the company's services going, in other words although I was ostensibly working against the strike, I did hope that the strikers would get as much of an increase as possible!

The president's job

The confusion about ownership furthermore distorts the function of the job of the president. A manager is an employee. However, strictly speaking, the job of the president is not that of an employee: the president employs: he puts to use the commitment of employees, stockholders, and customers.

To understand fully the implications of what I am saying, a distinction must be drawn between the role of the president and the person filling that job. The role of the president is independent of the board of directors; it is not something that is created, but arises out of the total field. As dynamic center, the role is necessary in order that the three forces, one of which is represented by the board, may stay in equilibrium and so allow the whole field to grow. These three forces have equal status within the total field. Growth will be accomplished provided that the appropriate action is taken to meet the situations that arise.

However, a distortion in the field is created because the board of directors representing just one of the forces within the field, appoints the person to the role. As well as being appointed by the board, this person is also conditioned to respond to the needs of the board by bonuses, stock options, and other profit-oriented rewards. The primary allegiance, therefore, of the president-as-person will be to the board of directors, while the president-as-role requires equal allegiance to all three forces.

One might protest that presidents, faced with the need to balance alternatives and to act in a way to optimize the return for the different forces making up the field, would find that they are unable to act at all. This is so if one is talking about the current way that presidents are expected to operate. Trying to balance the needs of the many dimensions of a company while being appointed, paid and with the possibility of being fired by just one of them, would be like trying to add up a column of figures on a calculator of which one of the keys is permanently held down.

Nevertheless, the objection that taking care of all the dimensions would overcomplicate the CEO's life has merit, albeit spurious, because undoubtedly, "we're in business to make a profit for the shareholders" does simplify, although quite simplistically, the problems that presidents have to deal with, as it eliminates many of the dilemmas. Given the nature of the limits within which he operates, (stockholder, employee and market and the wider environment) the criterion of the president's success is a balance of quantity, quality and value. By saying that the stockholder is king, the criteria are reduced to one single criterion: quantity only, represented by the bottom line. Any one who knows anything about accounting knows well that the financial statements of many companies are examples of modern art, and, like most modern art, are only vaguely, if at all, representative. The Enron financial statements are now among the better known of these works of art.[9] Furthermore, and this is as important a reason as any that I have given so far for the perpetuation of the myth, the bottom line gives the president's drive to be unique a simple but very effective way of being expressed: be the top performer — have the best bottom line — of Fortune 500!

Summary

From all that I have said, not only in this chapter but throughout the whole book, the way we look at corporations, what they are there for, who they serve and what value they have, must be given a thorough overhaul and corporate law in particular should be reviewed in the light of the current realities.

Such an overhaul is particularly important when one considers the increasing demand for higher ethical standards and even for the introduction of spirituality in the work place. According to Marjorie Kelly,[10] "The day-to-day action in ethics and CSR generally is at the level of management and staff. But ultimately who owns a firm —-and therefore how it is governed — will determine the company's deepest ethical core." In the next and last chapter of the book I will dwell further on the subject of corporate ethical behavior and corporate social responsibility that currently is receiving considerable attention.

Notes

1 Kelly, *The Divine Right of Capital*, pp. 35–36.
2 *Ibid.*, p. 22.
3 J. K. Galbraith, *The New Industrial State*, p. 84.
4 David A. Fausch, "Directors: Myth & Reality," *Business Week*, September 25, 1971. See also Mace Myles (1970) *Directors: Myth & Reality* (Boston: Harvard Business School Division of Research).
5 Kelly, *The Divine Right of Capital*, p. 51.
6 Fausch, "Directors: Myth & Reality."
7 *Ibid.*
8 *Ibid.*
9 See Kurt Eichenwald, *Conspiracy of Fools* (New York: Broadway Books, 2005).
10 Kelly, *The Divine Right of Capital*, p. 34.

CHAPTER NINETEEN

Creativity, Spirituality and Ethics in the Corporate World

In the foregoing I have offered a reality-based understanding of a corporation with which to replace the old mythological view that had its roots in the entrepreneurial stage of corporate development but which has now out-worn its usefulness. Entrepreneurs are justified in claiming that they are in business to make a profit. They are owner managers and also they often pioneer new ideas or new territory. Most modern corporations have evolved beyond the entrepreneurial stage into managerial and later still into investment capitalism. A new understanding based on the new realities of corporate life is essential to ensure that business serves the society from which it emerges and not simply one elite section of that society.

We hear much these days about spirituality, ethics and corporate social responsibility. For the most part, those advocating greater spiritual involvement, higher ethical standards and increased corporate social responsibility, are trying to graft new values onto a system that will either convert, or perhaps pervert, these values into a variation of its existing values or, more likely, reject the graft altogether.

Our behavior is a function of the situation in which we find ourselves and of our perception of that situation. As I showed in the first chapter of the book, perception is not simply a passive reception of information from the environment. It actively transforms that information in a creative process. While perception depends upon the situation, the situation depends upon our perception of it. I quoted Marjorie Kelly as saying, "The prime force [that drives the corporate world] is *systemic pressure, pressure that comes from the design of the system itself. The pressure to 'get the numbers' (generate profits for shareholders) is felt by CEOs or managers and enforced by them — but it originates* with the financial interests behind corporations."[1] As long as our perception of the system remains unchanged we are powerless to introduce meaningful change.

Sam Gibara, Chairman and former CEO of Goodyear Tire, whom I also quoted, confirms this, "Although the perception is that you have absolute power to do whatever you want, the reality is that you do not have that power. As a person you may want to act one way, but as a CEO you cannot do that."[2]

I am suggesting that we perceive the corporate system in an entirely new way. I am not adding anything, nor am I taking anything away from what we know as the corporate system. I am simply suggesting that it be seen as a multidimensional whole rather than a univalent vector. Even saying that the root of corporate life is creativity, a constant theme throughout this book, is not new. However, within the context that I am placing it, it acquires a new significance and a greater importance. With a new perception a fundamental change of reasoning and behavior is possible.

The fact that creativity plays a central role in life becomes more important when we consider it within the context of corporate life, because it shares a common root with spirituality and ethics. A new meaning can now be given to the search for ethics and spirituality at work and a greater possibility arises of finding ways by which we can satisfy the needs that have prompted this search. One might protest at the idea that creativity is at the root of spirituality and ethics and point to the concentration camp gas ovens, instruments cunningly designed by the creativity of the inventors, and wonder how one could associate creativity with the spiritual? Insofar as creativity can serve demonic purposes as well as spiritual ones, it must surely be ethically neutral. Before I can answer this objection I must undertake an exploration of creativity, spirituality and ethics.

More on dynamic unity

Earlier I said that creativity arises from a single idea in two incompatible frames of reference. The single idea is the product of commitment, involvement, intentionality or will. I called this commitment 'dynamic unity'. When, in chapter one, I first introduced the term 'dynamic unity' I called it a transcendent dynamism, a drive towards unity, which transcends conscious mind and experience. Transcendent unity has been the subject of all the great religions.

The word 'transcendent' is a somewhat heavy one and it might be as well to demystify it as much as possible. When you go to the cinema you see a film. It may be full of action, struggles, love and hate. At the end of the film all that remains is the white light projected on to the screen. All that you saw throughout the whole film was modifications of the white light projected on to the screen, but you were not aware of this while you watched the film because the white light *transcended*, or went beyond, the action of the film. In the same way dynamic unity transcends experience even though all the drama and action of our lives are simply modifications of dynamic unity.

All religions are founded on the reality of dynamic unity. The Vedic hymns are some of the oldest extant religious texts dating back many thousands of years. They were the precursors of the religions that emerged in India. The hymns stress the important of what I am calling dynamic unity. According to them, "Divine and human forms of expression reflect in [their] own way that transcendent, hidden, unified principle of harmony and order that supports and directs the movements of all things."[3] In Sanskrit, the unified integrative principle is called *Rta*.

The Israelites, from whom Christianity obtained the basis for its beliefs, did not see God so much as a Supreme Being but as what I am calling dynamic unity. They did not have a word for 'thing' and the nearest that they got to our word for thing was *dabhar*. Dabhar means 'word' but it also means, 'to be behind and drive forward'.[4] Thorlief Boman, a Norwegian Hebrew and Greek scholar whom I am quoting, tells us that in dabhar "Jahveh [God] makes his essence known"; furthermore, "whoever has dabhar knows Jahveh."[5] In other words, 'to be behind and drive forward', or 'to drive forward that which is behind' — which could be a fine description of the power of dynamic unity — is the highest manifestation of God. The concept of God as a Supreme *Being* came into existence with the introduction of Greek thought into theology.

The connection of all this to creativity and work becomes clearer if we consider the spirituality of Zen Buddhism. Zen Buddhism is an ancient practice for the development of a spiritual and ethical life that had its inception in China in the 5th century CE. It ultimately spread to Korea, Japan, Cambodia, and Vietnam. It was in Japan that it acquired its Japanese name of 'Zen'.

Buddhism has its own understanding of dynamic unity. Herbert Guenther, a professor of Oriental studies at the University of Saskatchewan,[6] explains that according to Tibetan Buddhism, "The universe is not only intrinsically 'intelligent', but is also a self organizing whole of what superficially looks like a, or the, One." The name that is given to the dynamic self–organizing whole is the *Ground*, in Tibetan, *gzhi*. It "is the ground and reason for everything . . . [it] is thoroughly dynamic . . . [and] responsible for the variety of structures, things, and experiences that are said to make up Reality." In Zen this ground is called *ku*, which is "living, dynamic, devoid of mass, unfixed, beyond individuality or personality — the matrix of all phenomena."[7]

Zen and work

The ultimate in Zen practice is awakening, or *satori*. One cannot really say what this expression means, although provisionally one might say that it means to be at home in the transcendent. However, it should not be inferred from this that Zen is otherworldly. On the contrary the Zen masters affirm, "Every day mind is the Way." The 'Way' means both spiritual practice and the goal of spiritual practice. This means that according to Zen, our work, family life, and the time spent with friends are all the Way; they are all spiritual practice and are the ultimate meaning of spiritual practice. One Zen Master says, "Whether you are . . . drinking tea or eating dinner, at home with your wife and children, meeting guests, on duty in the office, attending a party or a wedding celebration [or active in any other way], you should always be alert and mindful of the Work, because all of these occasions are first-class opportunities for self-awakening."[8] To be alert and mindful of the Work is to be mindful of what you are doing: if at work one is mindful of what one is doing at work, one is alert and interested; if one is with one's family, one is mindful of one's family; in other words one is attentive and empathetic to them and their needs.

Work has always played a large part in Zen and in many of the Zen stories we find accounts of the Zen masters and their students at work in the fields. One of these stories concerns a very old Zen master, Hyakujo. Even though he was way past ninety years of age he continued to work in the monastery garden, weeding, hoeing, and pruning. Eventually his students became worried about him and felt that he should stop work. As he would not listen to their concerns they hid his tools. When the master discovered this he went to his room, locked the door and refused to come out. As he missed several meals in this way, his students again became worried and pleaded with him to come out to eat. He said, "Only on condition that you give me back my tools." When they relented and did so, he came out of his room saying, "A day of no working is a day of no eating." I believe St. Benedict gave a similar injunction to his monks.

Zen and creativity

The direct link between Zen spirituality and creativity is shown by the practice of *koan* study. One of the two schools of Zen, the Rinzai, uses koans as the basis of the practice. One of the more famous of these is the following: A Zen master held up a stick to his assembly of monks saying "If you call this a stick I'll give you thirty blows; if you say it is not a stick I'll give you thirty blows. What is it?" This Zen koan was used by Gregory Bateson to introduce the notion of a *double bind*, which means we are damned if we do and damned of we do not. I showed the double bind to be a characteristic of the dilemma, but it also underlies creativity. The two — 'If you do' and 'if you do not' — are incompatible frames of reference.

In a susceptible individual, according to Bateson, the double bind could, in the extreme, bring about schizophrenia. He said, however, that the double bind is also common to humor, poetry, and art. We have seen the part that ambiguity and conflict can play in work and creativity. The koans of the Zen master show us how to work with dilemma and conflict. They show how, by becoming one with dynamic unity, we may 'transcend' the basic dilemma or schism that lies at the very heart of our being which I spoke of in the first chapter of this book.

The connection between spirituality and creativity can also be seen in the profusion of creativity that religion has brought forth. One only has to think of the abundance of cathedrals, temples and churches, of the music and dancing, of the liturgies, ceremonies and rituals, that it has produced to realize what a potent impetus spirituality is for creativity.

Ethics and creativity

When I discussed the spectrum of thinking I contrasted ethical thinking with moral thinking. I also called moral thinking *ought* thinking: I ought to do this, I must do that, I should do something else. Such thinking asserts good over bad. It is based upon fixed rules called moral codes, and these are given in terms of black or white, 'thou shalt' and 'thou shalt not'. Ethical conduct on the other hand is thinking that is sensitive to the nuances of the situation, and this sensitivity comes out of a high tolerance for ambiguity and a keen awareness of wholeness and unity. Creativity too requires a high tolerance for ambiguity and it seems evident that an ethical solution is a creative one. However, the gas ovens in the concentration camps during World War two show that while creativity shares a common root with ethics and morality — dynamic unity — a creative *solution* is not necessarily an ethical one.

Ethical and creative solutions differ because as well as a high tolerance for ambiguity the ethical solution calls for a keen awareness of wholeness and unity. The wholeness and unity of a company is not just an empty wholeness, on the contrary this wholeness is a dynamic, multifaceted whole made up of a set of elements each of which is whole and each has its own interests and so each is in potential conflict with the rest. The product that is produced by the company provides a dynamic center by which these conflicting elements find harmony and unity. But this harmony and unity is attained only through the creativity and leadership of the management of the company. To the extent that this creativity enables management to balance equitably the expectations and demands of all the dimensions of the whole company, to that extent management is acting ethically. To see the company simply as a set of investors, who are interested in gambling with the company's stocks, is a completely unrealistic and abstract view in which ethics can play no part at all.

From the view that management's function is to balance the needs and expectations of all the elements that make up the whole, we can derive a workable scale of ethical behavior within the corporate system. As a company is able to balance the demands of its various dimensions so it finds its place higher on the ethical scale. The whole that is highest in the hierarchy of wholes is the biosphere, and fully ethical behavior would be behavior sensitive to and responsive to the needs of all life. Human wants are infinite and the ideal of satisfying all demands all the time is both unrealistic and impossible to achieve. However, as the poet Robert Browning said, "Our aim must exceed our grasp, or what is heaven for?"

Logic and creativity

To attain a spiritual, ethical and creative company we must change the way we think. Logical thinking is anti-life and anti-creativity. To see what I mean by anti-life, one only has to see the kind of theories that are now being promulgated about the evolution of life and about the mind, theories that are based upon the scientific method, which is very firmly rooted in classical logic. According to these theories human beings are machines and the mind is just a vast computer. This either/or way of thinking cannot deal with the subtleties and complexities of living systems, and a company has many of the characteristics of a living organism. Life is not logical nor is the way we live or manage companies. In logic one requires clear and distinct thoughts, and one's thoughts are very rarely either clear or distinct. In very limited circumstances, in the scientific laboratory and the philosophers' study, logic can be an immensely powerful instrument, but outside of that we need a much more flexible instrument to help us to think.

In the practice of Zen we are warned against the misuse of logical thought. For example, a Zen master warns,[9] " Conceptualization is a deadly hindrance to Zen practicers, more injurious than poisonous snakes or fierce beasts . . . Brilliant and intellectual persons always abide in the cave of conceptualization; they can never get away from it in all their activities. As months and years pass they become more deeply engulfed in it. Unknowingly the mind and conceptualization gradually become of a piece. Even if one wants to get away from it, one finds it is impossible." Some people think that this shows that Zen is anti-intellectual, but it is simply warning against binding the mind up in logical rules and conceptual definitions that are not appropriate to life situations.

The logical way of thinking, supported and reinforced by the education system, convinces us that dilemmas and ambiguities are anomalies and that reason and logic alone can resolve the problems and difficulties in life and at work. In the face of this, and lacking any alternatives, management development programs, emphasizing more seminars and training, come into being. The reasoning is that failure to cope comes from failure to do something because something has yet to be learnt. Yet it may well be that the failure is not in what we know but in the way we use, that is think about, what we know.

Furthermore, in the main, when seeking to improve our knowledge we do so using the same either/or way of thinking. The old dichotomies remain embedded and unexamined, and the fundamental basis of industry is unchanged: human beings are resources to be used in the service of giving a return on investment to the stockholder, and the market is to be exploited for the same reason. Because we fail to weigh issues, to truly ponder the basis of our malaise, our inclination is to apply band-aids to immediate and perceptible problems. Seminars, task forces, and research give piecemeal solutions that do not fit together, all of which generates new problems, more task forces, and more systems leading to more piecemeal approaches, and more friction. It also leads to less and less meaning.

From the logical point of view dilemmas are cause for deep despair because they are irresolvable. For example, Arthur Koestler wrote, "the schizo-physiology inherent in man's nature and the resulting split in our minds, the old paranoid streak in man combined with his new powers of destruction, must sooner or later lead to geno-suicide."[3]

Because Koestler could not see that the 'split in our minds' is not only the source of our destructiveness but is also the source of creativity and the way to a spiritual life, all that he could conceive of was a biochemical solution. He felt that only a pill could restore 'dynamic equilibrium'. He felt that we are all in a way biological freaks that have lost our way, and if one looks at things from an either/or point of view such a conclusion is justified. We are a mentally sick race, he said, and as such dead to persuasion. As no natural corrective remedy is available, science must provide it: "Nature has let us down, God seems to have left the receiver off the hook, and time is running out." To an increasing degree society agrees with Koestler and is placing its faith in biochemical solutions to life problems.

Never in history have we been dosed with so many bio-chemical solutions, and never in history have so many suffered from anxiety and depression. "According to the WHO depression will become the second cause of absence from work after cardio vascular illness by 2020." Rod Philips, president and CEO of a Toronto-based employee assistance program, agrees that stress leaves by workers are on the rise. "We know that stress was the 5th most common cause of short termed disability leaves in 1996. By 2000, it had moved up to third place," he goes on. "In Germany depression is so widespread that the government has recently taken to pepping up the Germans' morale with positive thinking adverts."[10]

Bio-chemical remedies ultimately will merely salvage human beings as bodies at the expense of the human as a whole, that is as body/mind/soul. If we eliminate conflict to salvage meaning, the remedy itself may become the disease. Society wants the biochemical pill to provide dynamic equilibrium; but dynamism itself is disturbing the equilibrium. Koestler, who advocated the pill solution, saw so clearly the shadow, but would rid us of it by turning out the light.

The schism, the 'split in our minds', has great relevance to industry. Without understanding it, no viable organization is possible, conflict will be seen to be mainly personal and non-productive instead of sometimes being the basis of creativity. We will organize to suppress conflict, which in turn will create non-productive conflict and territorial struggles. Global wars are the final outcome of interpersonal conflict, the kind of conflict encountered daily, much of which in fact is created by poor organization. The territorial struggles of the super powers are simply magnified versions of interdepartmental conflicts. Each company has its own power politics; managers used Machiavellian tactics long before they became aware that their shifts and maneuvers had such ancestry. Let us not waste time asking for whom the bell tolls; it tolls for us. Nor should time be wasted seeking who is tolling the bell — the rope is in our own hand. We must resolve our own schism before turning to resolve the conflicts in the world. Unless the conflicts within ourselves and at work are used creatively, we will have to abandon creativity altogether or perish.

Even at the most mundane level, the presence of conflict and our unwillingness and inability to deal with it creatively must be of concern to management. Just as animals attack the trees in each other's territories rather than attack each other, so managers do not attack one another's person, but overtly or covertly deliberately destroy each other's systems.

The amount of damage inflicted upon a company in this way is enormous, and as specialization and information interchange increase, while communication and participation decrease, this damage and its attendant costs, will also increase. Even regarding the company simply from the perspective of the profit that it generates, the fact that so much is needlessly damaged should be of great concern. Much of this damage might never occur were we to deal with the basic ambiguity, Koestler's 'schizo-physiology of man'.

However, before trying to work creatively with the contradictions, dilemmas and ambiguities within a company we must be at ease with them in ourselves. This is tantamount to saying that we must be at home with insecurity, uncertainty, and dissonance, and even with the anxiety that is their emotional counterpart, and from which most people flee. When at home in ourselves, we can more readily address the dilemmas within a company.

The way we think must be revised, and ambiguity seen as the rule and not the exception. Furthermore the logic that divides the world through believing that a situation has to have a logical or reasonable solution must be supplemented by a logic of ambiguity, and by a constant search for creative solutions. Reason alone is no longer enough. We must learn to harness the transcendent, dynamic unity, that which hitherto has been called the 'unconscious': the prime mover in creativity.

The celebrated biologist T. E. Huxley mused on one occasion: "Science seems to teach in the highest and strongest manner the great truth which is embodied in the Christian concept of entire surrender to the will of God. Sit down before every fact as a little child, be prepared to give up every preconceived notion, follow humbly wherever and to whatever abysses nature leads, or you will learn nothing. I have only begun to learn content and peace of mind since I have resolved at all risks to do this."[11]

John Keats, the Romantic poet of 19th century Britain, also made a case for absence of commitment to one resolution or another, when he talked about the value of *negative commitment* in creativity explaining it occurs, "when a man is *capable of being in uncertainties*, mysteries, doubts, without any irritable reaching after fact and reason"[12] (author's italics).

I defined creativity as a single idea in two or more conflicting frames of reference. Before the single idea arises one must "be *capable of being in uncertainties*, mysteries, doubts, without any irritable reaching after fact and reason," or, in Huxley's words, "follow humbly wherever and to whatever abysses nature leads." However negative commitment must be within the limits imposed by the dilemma, by the dissonance that the situation has produced. One of the draw-backs of brain storming and similar methods for inducing creative solutions, is that so often participants are encouraged to just let the mind go free, rather than let the mind go free within conflicting limits.

Carly Fiorina, the former CEO of Hewlett-Packard, said, "Invention — which is at the heart and soul of what HP has been about and must continue to be about — invention depends fundamentally on creativity. And creativity, I believe, springs from a diverse group of people talking about the possibilities. And when I say diverse I refer to people who look different, people who think differently, people who have different backgrounds, people who have different skills, people who have different styles. I believe *diversity is critical to creativity*. And I believe creativity is at the foundation of invention"[13] [emphasis added]. The view that I have offered of a company as a dynamic field under tension provides the possibility for such diversity and for creative encounters.

I have wanted to show that a company is an *organic* complex; it is alive and has its own laws and demands. Life is resilient and can cope with an enormous amount of abuse and punishment. But it eventually succumbs. The excesses of WorldCom, RJR Nabisco, Enron, the Hollinger Group, among others, is a wake-up call to all. Will we kill the goose that lays the golden eggs, or will we have the sense to see that all must benefit from commerce and industry, that these are our servants and not our masters, that the corporate system was made for human beings? Human beings were *not* made for the corporate system.

Notes

1 Kelly, *The Divine Right of Capital*, p. 52.
2 The film *The Corporation*.
3 William K. Mahony, *The Artful Universe* (New York: State University of New York Press, 1998), p. 1.
4 Thorlief Boman, *Hebrew Thought Compared with Greek Thought* (New York: Norton Library, 1960).
5 *Ibid.*, p. 67.
6 Herbert Guenther, *Wholeness Lost, Wholeness Regained* (New York: State University of New York Press, 1994), p. 2.
7 Philip Kapleau, *The Three Pillars of Zen* (New York: Weatherhill, 1966), p. 74.
8 Chang Chen-Chi, *The Practice of Zen* (London: Rider and Co., 1960), p. 74.
9 *Ibid.*, p. 71.
10 *The Gazette*, Monday, July 11, 2005, front page, *Workplace juggling act takes stressful toll.*

11   Quoted by Stephen Jay Gould, *Rocks of Ages: Science and Religion in the Fullness of Life*, p. 40.

12   Lionel Trilling, *The Selected Letters of John Keats* (New York: Anchor Books, 1951), p. 103.

13   http://<www.creativityatwork.com/articlesContent/whatis.htm>.

References

Anshen, Melvin "The Management of Ideas," *Harvard Business Review*, July–August 1969.

Ardrey, Robert (1966). *The Territorial Imperative* (New York: Dell).

Argyris, Chris "How Tomorrow's Executives Will Make Decisions," *Think*, November–December 1967.

Arnheim, Rudolph (1982). *Power of the Center* (Berkeley: California University Press).

Auletta, Ken (2001). *Greed and Glory on Wall Street: The fall of the house of Lehman* (Woodstock and New York: The Overlook Press).

Balkan, Joel (2004). *The Corporation: the pathological pursuit of money and power* (Toronto: Penguin).

Bennett, J. G. (1966). *The Dramatic Universe, Vol. III* (London: Hodder & Stoughton).

Bertalanffy, Ludwig von (1968). *General System Theory* (New York: George Braziller).

Bloom, Allan (1987). *The Closing of the American Mind* (New York: Simon and Schuster).

Boman, Thorlief (1960). *Hebrew Thought Compared with Greek Thought* (The Norton Library: New York).

Boulding, Kenneth (1962). *Conflict and Defense* (New York: Harper and Row).

Brown, Wilfred (1960). *Explorations in Management* (London: Heinemann).

Brown, W. (1965). "What is Work?" *Glacier Project Papers* (London: Heinemann).

Burrough, Bryan and Helyar, John (1990). *Barbarians at the Gate* (New York: Collins Business Essentials).

Carpenter, Edmund (1966). "Image Making in Arctic Art," in *Sign, Image and Symbol* (New York: Braziller).

Chang Chen-Chi (1960). *The Practice of Zen* (London: Rider and Co).

Copenhaver, Brian P (1992). *Hermetica* (Cambridge: Cambridge University Press).

Dawkins, Richard (1988). *The Blind Watchmaker* (Harmondsworth: Penguin).

Drucker, Peter (1969). *The Age of Discontinuity* (New York: Harper and Row).

Drucker, Peter *Our Top-Heavy Corporations*, interview in *Dun's Review*, April 1971.

Eichenwald, Kurt (2000). *The Informant* (New York: Broadway Books).

Fausch, David A. "Directors: Myth & Reality," *Business Week*, September 25, 1971.

Ferguson, C., "Coping with Organization Conflict," *Innovation*, No. 29, March 1972.

Flew, Andrew (1975). *Thinking about Thinking* (Glasgow: Fontana).

Friedman, George (2004). *America's Secret War: Inside the hidden world struggle between America and its enemies* (New York: Broadway Books).

Galbraith, J. K. (1971). *The New Industrial State* (Boston: Houghton and Mifflin).

Garvin, David A. and Roberto Michael. A. "What you don't know about making business decisions," *Harvard Business Review*, September 2001.

Glass, James M. (1989). *Private Terror/Public Life: Psychosis and the Politics of Community* (Ithaca: Cornell University Press).

Guenther, Herbert (1994) *Wholeness Lost, Wholeness Regained* (New York: State University of New York Press).

Horney, Karen (1937). *The Neurotic Personality of Our Time* (New York: Norton).

Jaques, Elliott (1961). *Equitable Payment* (London: Heinemann).

Jaques, Elliott (1996). *Requisite Management* (Arlington: Cason Hall).

Jaques, Elliott "Industry's Human Needs," *Management Today*, May 1970.

Jung, G.C. tr. R. F. C.Hull (1953). *Psychology and Religion West and East* (London: Routledge Kegan and Paul).

Kapleau, Philip (1966). *The Three Pillars of Zen* (New York: Weatherhill).

Kelly, Marjorie (2003). *The Divine Right of Capital* (San Francisco: Berrett-Koehler).

Koestler, Arthur (1964). *The Act Of Creation* (London: Pan Books).

Koestler, Arthur (1967) *The Ghost in the Machine* (London: Pan Books).

Lamouche, Andre (1963). *Le Principe de Simplicité dans les Mathematiques et les Sciences Physiques* (Paris: La Colombe).

Levinson, Harry (1968). *The Exceptional Executive* (Cambridge, MA: Harvard University Press).

Levitt, Theodore "Marketing Myopia," *Harvard Business Review*, July–August 1960.

Lewin, Kurt, ed. Dorwin Cartwright (1951). *Field Theory in Social Science* (New York: Harper Torch Books).

Livingston, J. S. "Myth of the Well-Educated Manager," *Harvard Business Review*, January-February 1971.

Lonrenz, Konrad (1964). *Man Meets Dog* (London: Penguin).

Lovell, Jim and Kluger, Jeffrey (1995). *Apollo 13* (New York: Pocket Books).

Low, Albert (1993). *The Butterfly's Dream* (Boston: Charles E. Tuttle).

Low, Albert (2001). *Creating Consciousness* (Oregon: White Cloud Press).

Low Albert (2008). *The Origin onf Human Nature* (Portland and Brighton: Sussex Academic Press).

Mahony, William K. (1998). *The Artful Universe* (New York: State University of New York Press).

Maritain, Jacques (1955). *Creative Intuition in Art and Poetry* (New York: Meridian Books).

Maslow, Abraham (1962). *Towards a Psychology of Being* (New York: Van Nostrand).

May, Rollo (1967). *Psychology and the Human Dilemma* (New Jersey: D. Van Nostrand Co).

Mircea, Eliade (1961). *Images and Symbols* (London: Harvill Press).

Montague, Ashley (1965). *The Human Revolution* (New York: Bantam Books).

Muenzinger, K. F. (1942). *The Psychology of Behavior.* (New York: Harper).

Nadeau, Robert and Kafatos, Menas (1999). *The Non-local Universe: The New Physics and Matters of the Mind* (New York: Oxford University Press).

Rice, A. K. "Individual Group and Inter-Group Processes," *Human Relations,* Vol. 1, pp. 565–84. 22, No. 6, December 1969.

Riesman, Paul (1965). "The Eskimo's Discovery of Man's Place in the Universe," *Sign, Image and Symbol* (New York: Bantam Books).

Roberts, Benadette (1984). *The Experience of No-self* (Boston: Shambhala).

Sanders, Barry (1995). *A is for Ox* (New York: Vintage Books).

Selye, Hans (1956). *The Stress of Life* (New York: McGraw-Hill).

Spengler, Oswald (1932). *The Decline of the West* (London: George Allen and Unwin).

Stone, Irving (ed) (1937). *Dear Theo: Autobiography of Vincent van Gogh* (New York, Signet).

Von Bertalanffy, L. (1976). *General Systems Theory: Foundations, Development, Applications.* (New York: George Braziller).

Wagener, Daniel M. (2002). *The Illusion of Conscious Will* (Cambridge, MA: The MIT Press).

Walker A. H. and Lorsche, J. W. "Organizational Choice: Product vs. Function," *Harvard Business Review,* Nov.–Dec. 1968.

Watson, J. B. (1930). *Behaviorism* (Chicago: University of Chicago Press).

Index